ROBERT BATEMAN

100 GREAT SPORTSMEN

Carousel Editor: Anne Wood

TRANSWORLD PUBLISHERS LTD
A National General Company

100 GREAT SPORTSMEN

A CAROUSEL BOOK 0 552 54015 3

First publication in Great Britain

PRINTING HISTORY
Carousel edition published 1972

Copyright © Robert Bateman 1972

Carousel Books are published by Transworld
Publishers Ltd.,
Cavendish House, 57–59 Uxbridge Road,
Ealing, London, W.5

Made and printed in Great Britain by
Cox & Wyman Ltd., London, Reading and Fakenham

100 GREAT SPORTSMEN

Not *the* 100 great sportsmen – for no two
people's list would be the same – but a
book about one hundred people who have
been swifter, stronger or more powerful
than their competitors.

Also by Robert Bateman

ARCHIE — YOUNG DETECTIVE
MYSTERY FOR ARCHIE

and published by Carousel books

CONTENTS

ACKNOWLEDGMENT

Acknowledgment is made to the following for permission to reproduce photographs: World Sport; Central Press; The New Zealand High Commission; The Hungarian Embassy; The Swedish Embassy; The Australian High Commission; The French Embassy.

INTRODUCTION

Swifter than . . . stronger than . . . cleverer than . . .

These are the talents that single out the great from the also-rans in sport.

This book contains brief stories of the setbacks and achievements of a hundred of the 'greats'. Not *the* hundred – for it would be possible to find another hundred, and another, and another, all with every right to be considered great.

Most of them were selected not solely for what they achieved, but for the fact that in so doing they helped to broaden the understanding of the sports in which they competed, and have left us not only records but also standards of sportsmanship against which we can measure our own performances. Most, too, are not current heroes. Only a fortune teller could say with certainty that a sportsman in today's headlines will become a name to be remembered.

JESSE OWENS

'I'LL try for the world record,' he said.

The 21-year-old American with the ebony-coloured skin had equalled the world record for the 100 yards only ten minutes earlier. Now he was putting his handkerchief down beside the long jump pit to mark the existing world record. The big crowd at Ann Arbor in Michigan heard over the loudspeakers what he was going to attempt, and waited in hushed excitement as he slowly walked back for his run up.

Jesse Owens flashed down towards the pit, rose and skimmed onwards, flexing his legs forward, to land at 26 feet 8½ inches, beating the record by more than six inches, and setting a new one that lasted for a quarter of a century!

Another ten minutes went by, then Owens set a new record for the 220 yards, and also 200 metres. Less than half an hour later he did the same in the 220 yards low hurdles, with the metric record thrown in again for luck.

No other man in history has ever set five world athletics records in one day.

But few athletes have had such good reason.

Jesse Owens was a very small boy when he watched his father and mother pack up their few battered possessions to move north from the cotton fields of Alabama. He was one of eleven children. They arrived at Cleveland, Ohio, with new hopes – but when the great trade slump came in 1929 they were soon on the verge of starvation. Often the only money coming in was the small sum Jesse earned helping in a cobbler's shop after school hours.

Jesse Owens made a vow. Somehow – and he had not the faintest idea how – he was going to see that when the family grew up his parents did not still have to struggle in their old age.

Each day after school he ran to his job.

It was primitive training, pounding along the pavements, but it won him races at school. Universities, always keen to snap up a promising athlete, studied his progress. Twenty-eight of them competed to have Jesse as a student! Suddenly he saw ways in which he could make his vow come true. At Ohio University he was able to run, study, and also do a job which enabled him to send money home.

After his magnificent day at Ann Arbor, he was picked for the United States team for the Berlin Olympics of 1936. There, in front of a huge crowd, he won the 100 metres, the 200, and the long jump, also ran in the winning relay team.

With the cheers still ringing in his ears, Jesse Owens then achieved the promise he had made. He turned professional. He would run against anybody or anything for money. In Cuba, he ran against a horse! Money poured in, because anywhere in the world the name Jesse Owens on a poster meant that the crowds would flock to a meeting. He bought a new house for his parents, and invested his money so that neither he nor his family ever had to worry again about unpaid bills or where the next meal was coming from.

As late as 1955, Jesse Owens was still running. And every four years, at the Olympics, heads turn and arms wave when he takes his seat in the stands. Sprinters and long jumpers remember his achievements, and wonder if they can ever hope to do more themselves.

MATTHEW WEBB

The vicious seas slammed into the flank of the little sailing boat, and spray covered the men peering anxiously to starboard in search of a tiny black dot in the water.

It was an important dot – a human being, struggling to be the first man ever to swim across the English Channel.

Nowadays the Channel is swum every year, with a fleet of escort boats with strong engines which can bring them alongside in a matter of seconds if a swimmer gets into trouble. But the only escort for Captain Matthew Webb on 24th August, 1875, was one cockleshell of a boat which was in almost as much danger from the rough seas as Webb himself!

Webb had begun with a spectacular dive from Dover Pier. He was a short, strongly-built man, already the holder of a medal for trying to rescue a drowning sailor in mid-Atlantic. Now, with his body smeared with grease as a protection against the cold, he was fighting his way across against weather which grew steadily worse with every hour that passed. He swam breast stroke, as most swimmers did in those days. After five miles a cup of beer was handed down to him, then beef tea, and a spoonful of cod liver oil.

Then, after eight hours, he let out a yell of agony.

'Cramp!' exclaimed one of the men in the boat. 'Quick! Get alongside or he may go under.'

But when they reached Webb, it was not cramp which was causing the trouble. He had been stung on the shoulder by a jellyfish, and his arm was so numb that he was keeping himself afloat by treading water. A gulp of brandy restored his circulation, and he swam on.

At dawn, with the wind increasing, the seas broke over him, and the boat was swept so far away from him that if he had given up there would have been little hope of rescuing him. Then, suddenly through the murk and spray, he saw the French coast only 200 yards away. But he was swimming so feebly now that there seemed no chance he could make it.

What spurred him on was a shout from the boatmen. With a sounding line they had found the water was only seven feet deep – that in a few more yards he would be able to touch bottom and walk the rest of the way! Webb waved back, felt for the shingle with his feet, stumbled, and went under. Slowly, tottering, he came up again and staggered the last few yards to dry land.

Webb's time was 21 hours 45 minutes. He was a national hero.

It was 36 years before the Channel was swum again – and 59 before his record was broken!

BOBBY CHARLTON

The England team ran on to the field in Mexico for their quarter final tie with West Germany in the 1970 World Cup. The small crowd of ardent England supporters who had travelled thousands of miles for the World Cup Finals gave a cheer not only for the team, but also specially for Bobby Charlton, for by playing in this match he had beaten the record of 105 England caps set up a few years earlier by Billy Wright.

Bobby Charlton was one of the few Manchester United players who walked out of the Munich Air Disaster of 1958 alive, and since then he has won a World Cup Winners' Medal, a European Cup Winners' Medal, an F.A. Cup Winners' Medal, two F.A. Cup Finalists' Medals, and also Medals for United's League Championship victories. In 1966 he was first voted Footballer of the Year in England, and then European Player of the Year.

Joined by his brother Jackie, he played a major role in

England's World Cup victory in 1966. But perhaps the pinnacle of his career was his performance on the Wembley turf two years later, after which he led Manchester United up the steps to receive the European Cup. United beat the powerful Portuguese League Champions, Benfica, by four goals to one, and Bobby scored two of them. His first was a glancing header – an unusual shot for a man whose speciality has been powerful drives, usually close to the ground. It was this kind of powerful volley, in fact, which gave him his second goal – a lightning one from close range which gave no chance at all to the Portuguese goalkeeper Henriques.

Bobby Charlton has one further claim to fame. In all his years of football up to the time of writing, he has never been sent off by a referee. In the 'needle' football of the sixties and seventies, this is a notable achievement.

Edmund Hillary (right)

EDMUND HILLARY

THE tall, lanky New Zealander had been within 800 feet of the top of Mount Everest once before. So now, on the morning of 29th May, 1953, he was a very determined man indeed. All the massive preparation of a major expedition, starting from the foothills more than 28,000 feet below, had gone into placing him in his present position in the freezing cold just short of the summit of the world's highest mountain, the massive Himalayan peak which had never been climbed.

The sport of mountain climbing had always fascinated him – as it had his companion, the Nepalese mountain guide, Sherpa Tenzing Norgay. And as he woke up, at 3.30 a.m. in the primitive top camp not far short of the summit, he realized this was going to be the climax of his climbing career – if courage, and strength, and oxygen all held out.

But there was an immediate setback. Hillary had forgotten to put his boots inside his sleeping bag, and they were frozen as hard as iron. It took an hour to warm them enough to be worn. They ate a rough and ready breakfast, and then set off at 6.30.

The climb was an almost vertical white wall. One false step would not just mean the end of the attempt, but also the end of both their lives. They struggled upwards, inch by inch, to what is known as the south summit, 300 feet below the highest peak which was their target. Between the two lay a narrow, steep ridge of ice and rocks.

Roped together, 30 feet apart, they moved on towards the tantalizing peak which seemed to come no closer in spite of all their efforts. Hillary looked at his watch. It was 11.15 – they had been climbing for $4\frac{3}{4}$ hours.

They came to a snow slope – and suddenly Hillary grinned at Tenzing. For this last short stretch would be easy – and beyond it, only 30 feet away – was the peak!

According to Tenzing, it was Hillary who stepped on to the top just ahead of him – the first man on the peak of the world's highest mountain. The sun was shining from a bright blue sky above their heads. It was exactly 11.30 in the morning. They shook hands, and hugged each other in triumph, then thrust an axe into the snow with four flags attached, those of the United Nations, Great Britain, Nepal, and India.

News of the success reached Britain just in time to coincide with the Coronation of Queen Elizabeth the Second!

BABE DIDRIKSON ZAHARIAS

In men's sport there have been plenty of great all-rounders, but women seldom become famous the whole world over for success in a wide range of events. One exception is the girl who was once described as 'the athletic phenomenon of all time' – Babe Didrikson Zaharias.

At school in Texas in the nineteen twenties, she was the strongest of all her classmates by the time she was twelve – and the class included boys! But she was not heavily muscled. One writer described her as 'beautifully built, hard, and supple, with an almost feline grace of movement when she walked.'

It was when she ran, and jumped, that the grace of movement was not only marvellous to watch but also shatteringly effective against all opposition. She was only 17 at the time of the Los Angeles Olympics in 1932, but she won the 80 metres hurdles in 11.3 seconds, won the Javelin with a distance of 143 feet 4 inches, and was second in the High Jump at 5 feet 5 inches. Promptly – just to show that these three events did not exhaust her range – she went on tour with an All-American Basketball team, of which all the remaining players were men! Twice she was named the All-American Basketball Forward of the year.

At this stage it looked as though she was running out of worlds to conquer. So she branched out in an entirely new direction – golf. She won her first tournament in her own state of Texas. In 1946 she won the United States Women's Amateur Championship, and the following year became the first American to win the British Women's Amateur Championship. Immediately afterwards she startled the golf world by turning professional – one of the first women ever to do so. She won the American Women's Open title in 1948, 1950, and again in 1954 when she streaked home in a record 291 for 72 holes, to win by the tremendous margin of twelve strokes.

In 1932 her athletics successes had won her the title of the Greatest Woman Athlete of the Year; now her golf triumphs regained her the title. She was picked to hold it in 1945, 1946, 1947, and 1950, and in 1949 was voted the Greatest Woman Athlete of the Half Century.

Those who watched her 23 active years in sport tried to analyse her success. It was not brains – though she was a very intelligent woman. Nor was it strength – though she was strong. The general conclusion seems to be that it was courage, and a fighting determination to win which carried her to the top in everything she attempted.

Ferenc Puskas shoots, but ball is blocked by Swiss defence

FERENC PUSKAS

A THIN, weedy youngster who looked as though he hardly had the stamina to play soccer of *any* kind developed in the space of a few years into the man who ended England's proudest soccer record.

It was a November afternoon in 1953. England were at Wembley to defend yet again their record of never being defeated at home by a continental side. The crowd already felt uneasy; the reputation of the Hungarians had travelled ahead of them. They stared as the visitors came out on to the field led by their short, bulky captain, Ferenc Puskas. Few knew what had led up to this moment of triumph for him – leading his country's team into action at Wembley, the home of soccer. Few knew that he had begun his soccer with a home-made rag ball, kicking it up and down the street outside his family's cottage, watching carefully lest he damage his only pair of shoes.

The whistle blew, and within a minute the pattern of

play was set. It was clear that only fantastic luck could save England. Right from the kick-off, the powerful Hungarian forward line broke through – with Puskas running the ball at his feet, stopping suddenly, and then swinging it across to his centre-forward. The centre deceived the England centre-half, raced past towards the penalty area, and shot hard into the net.

Hungary were one goal up – and only sixty seconds had gone!

All eyes were now on Puskas, as he moved his men with military precision, and though after ten minutes England managed an equalizer, Hungary's forward line once again swooped down, regained the lead, and never lost it from that moment onwards. Then from far across by the right hand post, Puskas showed his own individual brilliance once more. He halted the ball, and used a trick he had developed even beyond the level developed by its inventor, Stanley Matthews. With the sole of his boot he moved the ball towards and then away from him, as though undecided what to do with it. The defence paused, uncertain whether to tackle or to wait a second in case Puskas passed.

Puskas did not pass. He continued the rolling of the ball for a fraction of a second longer, then changed feet and slammed in a shot which completely beat the goalkeeper.

His next goal was what looked like an idle touch of the ball as it was kicked into the penalty area. Puskas moved barely a foot, but diverted the ball unerringly into the net past the England goalkeeper. That made it four-one, and though England scored two more, so did the Hungarians. They left the field winners by six goals to three, and every one of those goals had been scored or 'made' by one man – Ferenc Puskas! No wonder Hungarians say he was the greatest player of all time.

GODFREY EVANS

THE man who in his day was called the world's greatest wicketkeeper was also the most entertaining player ever seen on a cricket field.

Godfrey Evans' family was cricket-crazy, and he first attracted attention when he turned out for 'The Evans Eleven' against a local village team in Kent – and pulled the Evanses out of trouble with a broad bat which reached nearly to his shoulders. The same pair of shoulders played the same defensive innings in the Adelaide Test against Australia in 1947, when Godfrey put in no fewer than 95 minutes' batting at a crucial stage of the game without scoring a run – but so entertainingly that the tough Adelaide crowd gave him a cheer. It was the same pair of shoulders which a few years later drove what is probably the only six-all-run (without over-throws) ever hit at Lord's.

First 'capped' against India in 1946, he made his first Test century in 1950, when joined by Trevor Bailey in a world record 6th wicket stand of 161 against the West Indies. This was cricket that hit the headlines. Evans played against five different countries in less than 18 months, and was already becoming famous for his red-lined gloves, his fantastic acrobatics, the unorthodoxy, the wild tangles of arms and legs from out of which would come a raucous 'Owzhat?' – and cricket's cheeriest grin if the appeal was turned down.

Picked as a Test selector for the 1950-51 tour of Australia, he celebrated the honour by a catch that rates for evermore as one which should have been impossible. This was in the notorious Brisbane 'sticky-dog' Test – when the pitch was so gluey after rain, with a hot sun beating down all day, that wickets tumbled faster than batsmen could put on their pads. Australia's Loxton cut a leg-break, and it hit Evans in the chest with tremendous force. As it rebounded off his ribs, Godfrey knocked it up, dived full length, and caught it as it fell!

His agility won him the world record for Test dismissals behind the stumps – and also got him out of trouble *off* the field. At Madeira, the rest of an MCC touring team hurried aboard the launch taking them back to their ship. But Godfrey Evans stopped to buy a huge bunch of bananas. 'Hold on a minute!' he yelled. Out in the harbour the ship hooted. The Portuguese launchmen waved their arms and headed out from shore.

So did Godfrey! Five feet eight of Evans hurtled from the quayside, bananas clasped tightly and legs thrashing the air!

It was a perfect one-point landing on the launch, with – as Godfrey put it – 'one foot slightly damp'!

MANIFESTO

A HORSE can be a great sportsman, too. In 1970 Nijinsky staked his claim to everlasting fame, but even his performances never equalled those of the amazing Manifesto – the steeplechaser they called 'the horse in a million'.

His biggest cheer was from the crowd in the Grand National of 1904. The roar went up as the winner passed the post, but doubled in strength for Manifesto as he finished ninth in the eighth Grand National of his career.

Even in his first National, run in fog so thick that the jockeys blundered their mounts into the jumps, unable to see them, Manifesto was fourth. He was then seven years old, and though in the following year's race he fell, in 1897 he removed any doubts about his quality by romping home an easy winner out of a field of 28.

The National of 1898 would have been his fourth, but for a mishap. A few weeks before the day of the race, Manifesto suddenly burst out of his box in a fit of springtime frolic and set out on an unofficial and private course of training that included a five foot hardwood gate. The result was a rapped fetlock which kept him out of the race. So terrified was he by what had happened because of his carelessness, Manifesto's stable-boy fled, changed his name, and was not seen again in the racing world for many years.

But in 1899, Manifesto won again. Many people expected him to win in 1900, but he was given 6 pounds extra weight to carry, and this proved enough to pin him back to third place – as it did in his next two races, those of 1902 and 1903. Finally, at the ripe old age of 16, he still managed to finish ninth in 1904 out of a field of 26.

It is a record which will probably never be equalled. Out of eight attempts he finished the course seven times, won twice, was third three times, and ninth at an age when most horses have long since retired.

Statue of Paavo Nurmi

PAAVO NURMI

In 1952, when Finland was host nation for the Olympics, the torch was carried into the arena by a lean, grey-haired runner in his fifties. He was still well remembered, for two leading young distance runners in the French team, watching his firm stride, grinned at one another ruefully. And one said, 'It's a good thing Paavo Nurmi isn't still racing. I believe he could beat us even now!'

It was 32 years earlier that Paavo Nurmi first created a sensation in athletics. He was virtually unknown when he turned out for Finland in the 1920 Olympics at Antwerp. He took second place in the 5,000 metres, then made a clean sweep of the longer distances by winning the 10,000 metres, the 8,000 metres cross-country, and contributing to the Finnish success in the 10,000 metres team race.

Four years later, in the Paris Olympics, he won over all distances from 1,500 metres to 10,000. So complete was his mastery that only 2½ hours after winning the 1,500 metres he was on the track again, winning the 5,000 – a feat followed by a record in the 3,000 metres team race, and also in the 10,000 metres cross-country.

This 10,000 metres cross-country was undoubtedly his greatest race. Veterans of athletics in the nineteen-twenties call it 'The Battle of the Sun', for Paris was going through a heatwave, with tropical temperatures and humidity. The 10,000 metres is a 'killer' distance in such conditions. Two dozen of the runners finished up in hospital. The only competitor who re-entered the Colombes Stadium looking as fresh as when he started was Nurmi. Even the crowds were exhausted by the heat, but they rose to their feet and cheered Nurmi for his superb fitness and endurance.

In the 1928 Olympics at Amsterdam Nurmi won the 10,000 metres again, and this brought his Gold Medal total to nine – a world record.

In all, Nurmi set up 24 world records over distances ranging from the mile to 20 kilometres. His efforts spurred other Finnish runners who had trained with him, and this small nation remained a powerful force in international running for many years after his retirement.

C. B. FRY

'IF it's sport, then I'll try it.'

That must have been the motto of C. B. Fry at the height of his career, seventy years ago.

As a County and Test cricketer, Fry was outstanding. He once knocked up six centuries in a row for Hampshire – and that was in the days when cricket was a game of real aggression, in which bowlers struggled to get wickets, not just to keep the scoring rate down.

When Fry was not engaged in a County game or one of his 26 Test matches, he played Rugby Union for Oxford University, Blackheath, and Barbarians, also Soccer for Oxford, Corinthians, and the League club, Southampton. Sometimes it must have been a confusing existence, for on one occasion he played in the Cup Final on Saturday and went on to score 78 in County cricket on the Monday!

As a high jumper and as a sprinter, he was in championship class, and could also produce an amazing burst of speed at the end of a long gruelling steeplechase. Furthermore – to show once and for all what sort of man he was – he equalled the World Long Jump record of his day.

He had not even intended to compete. He was resting in the changing room when the event began. He dragged off his sweater in response to a sudden challenge, put down the cigar he was smoking, and ran to the long jump pit.

A minute or two later, having equalled the World

Record, he came racing back to the changing room with
an anxious look on his face.

But C. B. Fry need not have worried.

His cigar had not gone out!

CRAIG BREEDLOVE

A LONG, lean monster scarcely recognizable as a car streaked across the bleak salt flats, jet driven at a speed which a few years ago would have been possible only in the fastest aeroplane.

Then a cheer went up – for once again Craig Breedlove had set a new World Land Speed Record, of well over 600 miles an hour.

Until the nineteen-sixties, Land Speed Records were for direct drive cars. But while Britain's George Eyston, Sir Malcolm Campbell, and Donald Campbell kept up a British monopoly for these, a small boy in America, Craig Breedlove, spent all his spare time drawing pictures of cars which he felt sure could outspeed them. When he left school he moved from job to job, always with cars, to learn everything he could about power, steering, suspension, and streamlining. And while he was doing this he kept up a constant bombardment of letters and phone calls to the American motor industry, asking for their support.

Eventually they gave it.

When he made his first record breaking run in his pure jet car, Spirit of America, in 1963, the watchers held their breath. Pure jets are difficult cars to drive. Their power is sheer blast from the back, not connected to the wheels. Nobody knew what special problems there would be once such cars reached high speeds.

But Craig Breedlove had developed driving techniques to anticipate these problems. He came sailing over the line with a world record of 407 miles an hour.

The motor firms which had backed him were more than satisfied.

But not Breedlove. He was already talking of 600 miles an hour. He took Spirit of America back to the workshops. The work of improving the car was spurred on by rivalry from another American, Art Arfons, who pushed up the record to 536 miles an hour.

Breedlove rushed Spirit of America to the course at the Bonneville Salt Flats in Utah, and made a new record of 555 miles an hour.

Arfons raised it to 576!

It was then that Breedlove achieved his ambition – with a speed of 600, which he has since raised far higher. And just to keep the records in the family, he let his wife Lee take Spirit of America out and raise the Women's World Record to 332!

STANLEY MATTHEWS

The F.A. Cup competition produces its heroes every season. But it seldom has a hero who is cheered quite as much as the Man of the Year in the 1952–53 season.

Stanley Matthews was already known to millions who had never seen a soccer match. He was 38-years-old, a veteran of the Blackpool team, which was built round a goal-making plan of a right wing formed by Matthews and the ex-Newcastle player, Ernie Taylor.

Blackpool faced Bolton Wanderers at Wembley in their third Cup Final in six years. Both their players and their supporters had the same grim thought as the game began – that it had to be now, or never. It was the same little group of players which, year after year, had brought them through to the Final. In soccer terms, all of them were now old men. If they could not win now, the chances were that they never would.

A goalkeeping error made it 1–nil against them right at the start of the match. Only a chancy shot by Stanley Mortensen put them on level terms again.

Relief was short-lived. Bolton whipped in two more goals to make it 3–1, and the situation looked desperate.

Then Blackpool started to play the pattern of football for which the team had been designed. Every time they got the ball, out it went via Taylor to Matthews, for what had been thrilling the crowd for twenty years – those amazing runs down the touchline, outwitting defender after defender with cunning footwork, until he reached a position from which a centre would find waiting marksmen.

Against modern defensive tactics, it is a system which seldom works today. But it worked in 1953. In went the centres, in went the shots, over and over again. Eventually it *had* to succeed.

It did.

But not until Matthews suddenly changed his tactics. He held on to the ball much longer, and his centre, when it came, was almost into the goalmouth – a gift for Mortensen to tap in past the keeper.

Back went Taylor and Matthews to the pattern as before – but with the score now 3–2. A brilliant kick, curving round the line of Bolton defenders, made it 3–all.

Then, with less than a minute to go to the final whistle, out went the last pass to Stanley Matthews. The yell from the crowd of 100,000 was deafening. The Cup was almost in Blackpool's grasp – and so was the Cup Winners' medal which had been Matthews' greatest ambition. Down the wing he went, tricking his way past two players. Wearily the Bolton defence struggled into position, but the pass came too quickly, and as Matthews slid on the green turf and went down at full length, he saw the ball slammed past the goalkeeper.

It was Blackpool's finest hour. And the finest for the player whose name was a household word in Britain for thirty years.

ROBERTO DE VICENZO

'I VERY lucky,' he laughed. 'I glad to won.'

It was not very good English, but Argentina's Roberto de Vicenzo had spent his life learning to be a top professional golfer, not a linguist. What he had just won was the British Open Championship of 1967. For twenty years he had been known as 'Mr. Near-miss'. In 1949 he was third. 'Better luck next time,' said the experts, tipping him as winner for the following year.

But they were wrong – de Vicenzo was third again. He was second in 1951, then third twice more. Year after year he proved himself a man would could play brilliant golf for round after round but who lacked the ability to crown his efforts with a superhuman final round.

In 1967, therefore, he came to Hoylake as a veteran trying yet again. And for once, the course was in the condition he knew well in Argentina – burned dry by weeks of hot sun. For years in the Open, his putting had let him down, but now, in these unusual conditions, it improved remarkably. People began to take serious notice when he went round in 70, while the title-holder, Jack Nicklaus of America, could do no better than 72.

Nicklaus recovered; at the half-way stage he shared the lead with Australia's Bruce Devlin, on 140; de Vicenzo, a stroke behind them, shared second place with three other players.

But it was the third day which brought the real drama. First, a brilliant 67 by the South African, Gary Player, shot him into the lead, but only a few minutes later de Vicenzo also completed a 67, which put him out in front for the first time – 67 was a new record for the course.

The final round was a battle amongst Player, de Vicenzo, and Nicklaus. The weather had remained dry and sunny; for the Argentinian, it had to stay that way.

It did. And no matter what miracles Jack Nicklaus pulled out of the hat in trying to defend his championship, de Vicenzo was now unbeatable. Long putts sailed neatly into the hole; drives sizzled straight down the fairway to the greens. Finally, along the fairway of the 18th, his progress was that of a conquering hero, leading a procession of the hundreds who had watched him fail in the past!

DENIS COMPTON

The crowd rose to their feet.

The great Denis was having his last innings, ignoring the agony in the knee that was ending his career, in order to entertain them one last time with bold strokes all round the ground.

To many of those who watched that game in 1957 it was an emotional moment. For they had also been there more than 20 years earlier, watching the young Denis Compton play his first innings for Middlesex, and had crossed over the river from Lord's to the Oval to see him hit 65 off New Zealand in his first Test. A year later, at Trent Bridge, they had seen him hit 102 against Australia.

When post-war county cricket began, Compton quickly became the most popular batsman in the country, for his brilliant strokes drew big crowds wherever he played. His partnerships with Bill Edrich provided some of the most exciting cricket ever seen. The only way either seemed likely to get out was to be run out – and they risked this constantly by sneaking runs off short strokes and overthrows. In 1947 Compton hit 3,816, with an amazing average of 90.85. The total included 18 centuries.

His winters as a footballer were just as successful. He won a Cup Winners' medal playing for Arsenal in the final of 1950 with his brother Leslie in the same team.

But then came trouble.

Suddenly every sports fan in Britain was talking about Denis Compton's knee.

The trouble had begun long ago, in a soccer match before the war. Compton had a successful operation to put right a cartilage injury, and the knee was only occasionally painful until 1947. Then a long summer of cricket on bone-hard grounds brought the agony back again. Doctors discovered a fragment of loose bone in the knee joint; they operated, and removed it. This gave the knee a new lease of life which lasted until after the 1950 Cup Final.

But then came a third operation, and it was less successful. He had to give up soccer, and there was continually the threat of his also having to give up cricket. Doctors advised him to retire.

Instead, Denis Compton went on to more Test series, not only as a batsman and reliable man in the field, but also as a spin bowler – changing to his left hand to deliver his dreaded 'Chinaman' – the end, unpredictable ball that wrecked many an innings. But by 1955 his knee had to be held in iron calipers between innings. Doctors operated again; one said afterwards, 'We had to put in 17 stitches. How anybody has the guts to play cricket with a knee like that beats me!'

Eventually it even beat Denis. And so in 1957, with nearly 39,000 runs behind him – 5,807 of them in 78 Tests – came that retirement match, with the bold hitting that proved the guts could still be summoned up one last time for the crowds who had cheered his long career!

BERYL BURTON

BRITISH cycling stars are rare, so when she became World Road Race Champion it was a special triumph for Beryl Burton. She had not only had to overcome lack of support, but also lack of facilities.

In her early thirties, blonde, stockily-built, Beryl Burton does not look like a world champion, and for most of the year, in fact, she is – or thinks of herself as – a Leeds housewife with a job in a market garden. But when the big events come round, Beryl Burton is always there. In Britain, rivals have appeared on the scene to challenge her supremacy, only to give up in despair.

When she was 17 she married a racing cyclist, and it was not long before he gave up his own career on the track to concentrate on training her. The tactics of cycle racing are as fine an art as those of running. The saving of energy for sudden spurts at the crucial moment, the lulling of opponents into a false feeling of security, the exact knowledge of each opponent's weakest points – these are the factors which win races. Only years of concentration can develop these tactics in the way Beryl Burton has done.

She has also conquered the great menace in all top-class sport – pre-race nerves!

When her opponents are waiting anxiously for the start of their race, moving about flexing their arms and legs, checking and rechecking their machines, jogging up and down, or holding forced conversations in which the laughter is strained with the tension, Beryl Burton will be found a short distance apart from the rest.

Usually she is sitting down, and anyone, such as a trainer, who is expert at judging nervous and muscular tension, would see complete relaxation.

This is because, long before a race, Beryl Burton has already worked out her tactics. For her, the worries are already over.

So, during the final minutes of waiting, until the final signal for the line-up, the world champion from Leeds settles down with knitting needles and a ball of wool!

MATT BUSBY

MATT BUSBY – nowadays Sir Matt – has had two brilliant careers in soccer. The first was as a Scottish international wing half, and as wing half in Manchester City's Cup-winning side in 1934. The second was as the man who at the end of World War Two was invited to become boss of a muddy field full of humps and bomb-holes, flanked by the rusty skeleton of a bombed and burned out stand.

The place was Old Trafford, and there was not much left of Manchester United's team, either, when he took it over.

Within a few years Matt Busby carried them to Cup and League success, and became Britain's most famous soccer manager.

Then, on 6th February, 1958, came the greatest team disaster in football history. The Manchester United team, with Matt Busby and a group of football re-porters, was leaving Munich airport for home when their

B.E.A. Elizabethan crashed. Twenty-three people were killed; others, including Busby himself, were seriously injured.

It looked like the end of what had become a Matt Busby and Manchester United legend.

But as soon as Busby could stand on sticks, he gave a press conference. United, he said, would recover. And they did, to reach the Cup Final only three months later. They were beaten, but so well had Matt Busby built up his reserves of players that in the following year they were second in the League, and a few years later they were winning both League and Cup.

Busby's recipe for success never varied. From the moment he went to United, he set about ensuring that every man would go on the field on Saturday afternoon with his mind clear of everything but football. He made the club into a kind of 'universal father'. If a player had worries about money, housing, schools, or his family, there was no need to sit at home and brood about them. Instead, he took them to the club, where the calm, level-headed Matt Busby listened carefully, and then somehow found a way of taking the burden off the player's shoulders.

For Matt Busby had discovered a secret – that top performers in any sport could *remain* top performers only by remaining single-minded – that a worried man cannot give of his best.

JOE LOUIS

'SEE here, boy,' they told him, 'professional boxing could make you rich. But cotton-picking never will.'

Joseph Louis Barrow knew they were right. The State of Alabama in the nineteen-thirties was not the world's easiest place for a cotton-picking negro to get ahead, and after winning the National Amateur Light-heavyweight title he had already headed for the north, where a dark skin was less of a handicap to a man aiming for the top.

His first professional fight, in a tough hall in Chicago, was against Jack Kracken, an experienced opponent who was also a favourite of the local fans. Joe Louis moved straight in the moment the bell went, and won by a knock-out in the first round. Before he had even climbed out of the ring his managers were excitedly planning a series of fights to build him up as the greatest heavyweight prospect of the twentieth century.

So began a year of rough, mauling fights against better and better opposition. In that year, Joe fought 12 times, and scored 10 knockouts. By the end of it, the name Joe Louis on a wall poster meant automatically that every ticket would be sold. For several years the crowds had seen only fighters, but here now was a boxer, a good-looking athlete of the ring who fought with his brains as well as his strength.

On 22nd June, 1937, in Chicago, Joe Louis knocked out James J. Braddock in the 8th round to become the first negro holder of the World Heavyweight Championship since Jack Johnson a quarter of a century earlier.

The dollars rolled in – nearly two million dollars at one fight alone. Joe's fans would pay fantastic prices to see him fight, and when he retired, in 1949, after defending the title 25 times and losing only one fight in his whole professional career, his earnings totalled only a little under two million pounds! He had fought and beaten every well-known heavyweight of the time, including Max Baer, Primo Carnera, Max Schmeling, Jack Sharkey, and Jersey Joe Walcott. But bad management, and heavy taxes, left him a poor man, and a year later he tried to make a come-back. Ezzard Charles beat him on points, and Rocky Marciano knocked him out. That was enough. But debts and taxes forced him into the sport most professional boxers despise – wrestling – until doctors warned him his heart was not as strong as it had been, and he must climb out of the ropes for the last time.

Boxing had not given Joe Louis financial security. But it had given him admiration – and the proud memory that he had never once been booed in the ring.

Nobby Stiles with Bobby Charlton

NOBBY STILES

A TOOTHLESS grin in the middle of a face wild with triumph and excitement – and out in front, the Jules Rimet Cup held aloft. It was Nobby Stiles, after England's 1966 victory in the World Cup, and the 100,000 crowd at Wembley yelled his name.

He has no enemies in England. But abroad it has been very different. In a European Cup semi-final for Manchester United against A. C. Milan the Italian crowd booed him before he had even kicked the ball. In Argentina, when United played Estudiantes, the home side printed the words, 'Nobby Stiles is an assassin' in the match programme. When the game began, Estudiantes went not for the ball, but for Stiles, and under a very strange interpretation of the rules, he was eventually sent off by the linesman for being offside!

But none of this enmity has affected his brilliance or his enthusiasm during his career with United. It included an F.A. Cup Winners' Medal, two League

Championship Medals and a European Cup Medal to
go with his medal for England in the World Cup.

A knee injury and loss of form in the autumn of 1970
signalled that his career in top class football was probably nearing its climax, but behind him are the triumphs
of 28 caps for England at a time when English football
was at its peak, and the respect and affection not only of
the home crowds and his team-mates, but also of his
League opponents.

CYRIL WASHBROOK

Shamefaced, 17-year-old Lancashire batsman Cyril Washbrook walked back to the pavilion. When a batsman has made a century, and he strolls back towards the cheering crowds, it is the shortest walk in the world, but when he has made a duck, the pavilion seems like a dot on the horizon!

And a duck was what Washbrook had achieved. He knew what was waiting for him in the changing-room – a frown like a thunder cloud from the 'boss', the old man of Lancashire cricket, Makepeace.

Cyril's knees went weak. He had been clean-bowled by an off-break. And that, Makepeace had said to him not once but a hundred times, was the greatest crime in cricket.

'Well? Where were your legs?' Makepeace asked him scornfully. '*Paralysed?*'

For the next week, Cyril Washbrook kept out of everybody's way. It was 1932 and he was trying to become a professional cricketer at a time when unemployment was at its height. He was scared of losing his job.

But fear brought concentration. In his second match for the county he played a faultless innings of 152. His cricket career unrolled ahead of him. After the war the Hutton-Washbrook opening partnership for England in Australia hammered runs off Lindwall and Miller – two of the fiercest bowlers in cricket history. A few years later, the partnership stood up to the equally devastating spin attack of the West Indies.

Late in his career, at the age of 41, Washbrook was brought back into the England side for a Test at Leeds and had the satisfaction of saving an innings which was crumbling badly in the hands of men 15 years his junior. Calmly, with the relaxation he had perfected many years earlier in the days of Makepeace's sarcastic criticism, Washbrook made 98. He had reached the top. Now he was holding out a helping hand to those struggling up towards it.

DORIS HART

The doctors stood round the two-year-old girl on the operating table. 'We'll have to amputate,' said one of them. He looked at the leg, twisted and powerless as the result of polio.

One of the other doctors shook his head. 'No,' he said. 'Better a crippled leg than none at all.'

That decision gave tennis one of the greatest Wimbledon champions. By the time she was six, Doris Hart was hobbling out into the garden of her home in America, to hit a tennis ball about with her brother as partner.

It was painful at first, and frustrating, too. Time and again, her weak leg let her down as she tried for a ball beyond her reach. But, as so often with someone physically handicapped, Doris's brain came to her rescue. What she could not manage by speed of movement, she achieved by quick thinking.

By the time she was 12, Doris had graduated far beyond back garden tennis. She was given expert coaching, and found herself winning local tournaments. At the age of 15 she was in the United States Junior Championships – always aware that when she missed a difficult ball, there were whispers behind her – 'The poor girl! If it wasn't for that lame leg, she'd have managed it.'

But she was one of the pair who took the Junior Doubles Championship. Doubles, the experts said, would be her limit. To prove them wrong, she won the Junior Singles at 17 and again at 18. She became ranked

Number 6 in America, and picked for the Wightman Cup team against Britain.

She reached the Wimbledon Singles final in 1947, at the age of 22. By now the crowds were used to the awkward walk, the sudden look of strain on Doris Hart's face if she had to leap for a virtually impossible shot. No longer were they giving her sympathy; they knew she did not need it.

She was beaten in the 1947 and '48 finals, and in the 1949 semi-finals, but in 1950 found herself on the Centre Court against her close friend Shirley Fry.

The spectators were hushed as Doris Hart moved about the court, unbelievably fast for one handicapped as she was. It was as if for 40 minutes the polio had never happened, and the leg was straight. So devastating were her serves, so unplayable her returns, that she won 6–1, 6–love!

Then, in partnership with Shirley Fry, she won the Doubles. This was a much tougher match; it seemed impossible she could then join Frank Sedgman of Australia in winning the Mixed Doubles. But she did!

Doris Hart had achieved one of the greatest successes possible in tennis – the Wimbledon triple!

JACKIE CHARLTON

Toe to toe in their pram, the two brothers watched village soccer at Ashington in Northumberland. It was no wonder their mother took them there on afternoon walks; she was the daughter of a noted goalkeeper, 'Tanner' Milburn, and her brothers George, Stan, Jimmy and Jack were all fullbacks in League soccer. Her cousin was Jackie Milburn of Newcastle.

Twelve years later Jackie Charlton heard Manchester United's chief scout, Joe Armstrong, tell his mother, 'Your boy'll be playing for England before he's 21!'

But Jackie knew he was not that boy. He watched his brother Bobby rise swiftly to the top. While Bobby was the star, Jackie was on Leeds' transfer list, with the prospect of dropping into Fourth Division football.

It was the arrival of Don Revie as Leeds' manager which changed all that. Revie showed Jackie how he had failed because of over-boldness on the field, how to control the impulse to go for a ball that could not be reached, and that being where he *ought* to be was more important than trying 'solo spectaculars' without the backing of his team mates. Suddenly Jackie was as big a star as his brother. Bobby was Footballer of the Year in 1966; Jackie followed him a year later.

In the 1966 World Cup final they joined forces, their main task being as 'feeders', guiding the ball and the play into areas where the German defence was momentarily weak. For them, there were no goals, but the immense satisfaction of helping to make all four in England's 4–2 victory.

In the years since then, Jackie Charlton has remained a mainstay in the Leeds team. And for the future, the prospects are bright. When Jackie's son was born, the baby's grandmother, still searching for more soccer talent, took one look at him and then smiled.

'There you are,' she said, 'he's got footballer's feet!'

EMIL ZATOPEK

IN the 10,000 metres race at the 1948 London Olympics, Heino of Finland was confidently expected to keep up his country's virtual monopoly – Finland had failed to win only once, in 1932, since the race was introduced in 1912. But on a grey, rainy London day, Heino's lead was gradually cut down by a mystery runner who many of the watchers could not even identify.

After ten laps, this 'dark horse' broke past Heino into the lead. Heino struggled to stay with him, and succeeded until lap 16. But then the unknown competitor – Emil Zatopek of Czechoslovakia, on his face the twisted grin of determination which became famous on every major track in the world – broke away, increased his pace, and completed the final laps so fast that he looked as though he was running a mile.

At the finish, he had improved the Olympic record by more than 15 seconds. And he went on from that to collect world records over distances ranging from 5,000 to 30,000 metres. By 1952, he reached his peak. Even to attempt the 5,000 metres, 10,000 *and* the marathon, all at one Olympics, is startling enough, but to win all three in Olympic record time is unique. Zatopek achieved this triple in the 1952 Helsinki Olympics, and continued his career for another five years before retiring with behind him such stupendous performances as running 38 races in succession without defeat!

When he left competitive athletics he devoted himself to his army job as a sports instructor. Again he was highly successful. Defeat came at last, not at the hands

of other sportsmen, but those of politicians. When the
Russians entered Czechoslovakia in 1968 he was one of
the many well-known people who openly defied them.

It cost him his career.

JIM LAKER

THERE are some sportsmen who need exactly the right partner to bring out the best in them. Such a man was Jim Laker, who bowled beautifully neat and compact offbreaks for Surrey during the long spell in the nineteen-fifties when they won the County Cricket Championship year after year.

On his own, Laker was notable, but in partnership with Tony Lock, he was terrifying. Against this double attack, even the most experienced batsmen faltered – men like Australia's Keith Miller and Ian Johnson. It was not that they failed against the pressure of an unvarying style, for the two bowlers were totally different.

The partnership's greatest day was 31st July, 1956, at Old Trafford. The match was the Fourth Test against Australia, which, if England could win it, meant they retained the Ashes.

Jim Laker, on the strength of taking 6 wickets in the First Test, 3 in the Second, and 11 in the Third, was given the job of breaking Australia's back. At the other end, Tony Lock took on the job of wearing out the batsmen's patience, ready for Laker to pounce.

And pounce Laker did! In Australia's first innings, he took 9 wickets for 37 runs. Aided by Lock's dismissal of opening batsman Burke, he had personally closed the innings.

Australia had to follow on, and in their second innings Laker and Lock bowled 106 overs between them. Of Lock's 53, no fewer than 30 were maidens, which so infuriated the batsmen that they promptly fell foul of Laker. Their first innings had ended at 84, and so, following on 375 behind, they were forced to go for runs, and with Lock 'shutting up' one end, they had no option but to hunt for runs off Laker.

Instead of getting runs, all the Australians got was the long trudge back to the pavilion! Laker took all 10 wickets, giving England victory by an innings and 170 runs, with just over an hour to spare. His 19 wickets in the game were the most ever achieved by any bowler in any first-class match.

But nobody forgot the less spectacular role played by Tony Lock. As newspaper and radio reporters crowded round him asking how he had done it, Jim jerked a thumb towards his partner. 'Don't forget Tony,' he said. 'I had him at the other end. He set 'em up for me!'

Dawn Fraser (left) with Lorraine Crapp

DAWN FRASER

'COME o-o-o-o-on, Dawnie!'

The loud yell from frantic Australians shrilled out across the Olympic swimming pool in Tokyo – sound which veterans of previous Olympics had heard before, at Melbourne in 1956, and in Rome in 1960. Dawn Fraser had won the Women's 100 metres freestyle final both times, for an Olympic double. Now she was trying to become the first woman ever to carry off the event three times.

Twelve years is a long time in swimming. Most world class swimmers reach their peak by the time they are twenty, and retire soon afterwards. A sprint swimmer of 27 is a rarity.

Even rarer is an Olympic competitor who takes part in a final only seven months after a serious injury. Dawn was one of four people involved in a car crash in Sydney in March 1964, which her mother did not survive. She, her sister, and a friend, were all badly injured, and Dawn had to have her neck in a special collar for weeks. At the time of the accident, she had just broken her 36th World Record. She had two ambitions left – the Olympic triple, and to increase her total of records to 40. Her superb physical condition and will to recover amazed Australia's Olympic selectors – and so, here she was, with the yell of 'Come o-o-on, Dawnie!' as she hit the water a fraction ahead of her seven rivals. Then, as she sped towards the turn, almost all the crowd, whatever their nationality, had taken up the shout. 'Dawnie! Dawnie!' The tragedy she had overcome, and her brave determination, overshadowed all national rivalry.

At the turn, however, Dawn was being shadowed closely by a young American, Sharon Stouder. Sharon was quicker away on the final lap, and for a brief spell both girls were level.

The cheering died a little. For there was no sudden recovery by the Australian. Yard after yard Dawn and Sharon were neck and neck. Then the cheer rose again as Dawn Fraser's experience and self-discipline brought her out in front once more. In taking the lead at a moment like that, every minute fraction of superiority counts; better breathing control, a minute twist of the hand to scoop out an extra teaspoonful of water with each stroke – it is details like these which win Olympic victories.

The result was in the balance until the last few yards. Then the cheering was redoubled; Dawn was the winner.

She had achieved her Olympic triple!

STUART MACKENZIE

FOR six summers at Henley — the world's greatest rowing regatta — an enormously tall Australian won that supreme event for solo oarsmen, the Diamond Sculls. To do so he had to beat the top men from America, Russia, Germany, and Britain.

What enabled him to do this was an almost unbelievably tough attitude towards sport, born of the fact that he had to live up to the standards set by two generations of champions. His grandfather was an Australian Test cricketer, and his father was the Australian Surfboard champion. After that, for Stuart Mackenzie to be anything less than a champion would have been unthinkable. So when he first took up rowing, he did so with the knowledge that he *had* to succeed.

Because the Thames is the Mecca of rowing, Stuart took on a job in Britain and settled at Henley. His popularity grew with the crowds — but not with officials. Traditionally, winners passed the Henley winning post 'eyes 'front'. Stuart would arrive grinning! Traditionally, whatever the weather, oarsmen wore the correct rowing kit. In freezing weather Stuart, however, turned out in a track suit.

One of his greatest victories came in the 1958 Diamond Sculls. He and his great rival, Y. Ivanov of Russia, were both so exhausted by the half-way stage in their race that it looked as though they would barely be able to finish, and then only in a very slow time for competitors of their calibre.

It was then that Stuart showed how his willpower could overcome the failure of his stamina. While Ivanov watched, unable to increase speed, Stuart began gradually to pull away, driven onwards by his immense will to win. He finally crossed the line no less than 22 lengths in front!

But winning by willpower imposes a terrific nervous strain. Stuart Mackenzie began to be worried by nervous illnesses. It was found he had a duodenal ulcer. An operation was not completely successful; nervous and stomach troubles started up whenever he had to compete in a big race.

Finally, in 1965, he found the answer. He went to America as professional coach to the oarsmen of Columbia University, a job in which he was able to pass on his knowledge and skills to others without ever again subjecting himself to the nervous strain which his body could not stand.

JOE DAVIS

Billiards and Snooker were becoming almost forgotten sports when television brought them back to public attention. What many people do not know is that they had been brought back once before – not from obscurity, but from disgrace! For fifty years ago billiard halls were in bad repute. When the police wanted to find criminals, billiard halls were on their list of likely places.

Then along came a fifteen year old who did not see why two great games of skill should remain in disgrace. Joe Davis was short, already rather plump, with smooth shining hair brushed down very flat, and the kind of eyesight that wins prizes at archery or shooting. At fifteen he was a brilliant amateur, and when he turned professional, big crowds were soon coming to watch him. They were not the petty crooks and pickpockets who had hung around the billiard halls a few years earlier; they were people who enjoyed playing both billiards and snooker at home, and who wanted to learn the technique of the master.

And Joe Davis certainly *was* the master! In 1927, with an old cue he had bought from a local rival, he won the professional championship. That cue, known as 'Old Faithful', travelled with him for more than 40 years, and won him four World Billiards titles – and finally, in 1963, the O.B.E. That cue cost Joe 7/6d, but so much money did it earn that he was able to do much of his playing not for his own profit but for charity. For example, thousands of people have paid to see him try to equal the World Snooker record he set up in 1955 – a break of 147, the maximum possible. It is an almost impossible task, because it involves potting every red ball, also the black with each of the reds, and all the colours. Thousands of pounds went to the Imperial Cancer Research Fund from the gate-money paid by the crowds watching Joe try to do so.

Joe also scored more snooker centuries than any other player – 687 – and when he retired from professional snooker in 1965, he left behind him a game which had become respectable, and which had not only proved itself capable of drawing the crowds but which also appealed to those sitting at home, watching the play on the television screen.

On the day of his retirement, somebody asked Joe what he was going to do now that he had played in his final tournament. Joe looked at the questioner as though he must be stupid. 'Why,' he said, 'I'm going straight home – to have a game of snooker!'

DAVE MACKAY

IN soccer, with fitness as important as skill, the greatest handicap for any man at the top is the one weak point against which he must always be on his guard. Sometimes called 'The Iron Man of Football', one of the ablest men in the game today, Dave Mackay discovered *his* weak point eight minutes after the start of a match for Spurs against Manchester United. He went for the ball, collided with an opponent, and went down, with a jab of agony shooting through his left leg. In hospital, it was found he had broken two bones.

He was only 28, with the prospect of many more years at the top. But, because of injuries, he had always been fully aware that his soccer career could end suddenly, so he had invested his money wisely in business. He was thankful for this, for he had nagging doubts about the way the bones were healing. Next season, in a reserve game designed to test his recovery, the leg gave way again. He missed the whole of the season.

The question he now asked himself was whether he would ever dare to play again without consciously safe-guarding his leg at every move. In July 1965 in a training game he swallowed his fears, and used his leg in a hard tackle, turning and twisting on it so that the newly-knitted bones had to take his full weight. To stay at the top, he knew, he must play exactly as he had always done, that the slightest concession to his weak leg would mean the difference between star quality in his play and the merely adequate.

So Dave Mackay took risks, and became an even greater player than before – and when his fastest days were over, moved from Spurs to Derby, to restore the fortunes of a team which needed most of all the steadying influence of an expert in the half back line. Medically, no broken leg can ever be as strong as it was before, especially when it has been broken twice. But in soccer there *can* be a victory of mind over matter, and Dave Mackay, moving a little more slowly now but master-minding every Derby attack, has remained a star, in a different role.

BOBBY MCGREGOR

If you do not reach your peak in swimming before you are twenty, the chances are that you will never be a world champion.

That was what haunted Scotland's Bobby McGregor. He was already past twenty, and had become renowned all over the world as the 'hot breath on the neck' of Don Schollander, world record holder for the short distance free-style events. Their rivalry had begun when Schollander beat him by a fingertip in the Tokyo Olympics in 1964. An Olympic Silver Medal is not to be scorned, for it is virtually a badge to say you are the second fastest man in the world. But McGregor had set his heart on a Gold.

Training at home in Falkirk for the 1966 Commonwealth Games he tried to puzzle out why his swimming career had brought three Silvers, but never a Gold. Nerves was one thing. The other was an unaccountable slackening of pace in the last ten yards. Knowing is often conquering; he was confident when he went to the Games – but again he could only win a Silver!

It was then that Bobby McGregor became an angry man. Less than a month later, he went to the European games in Holland. Against the Russian, Leonid Ilyichev, his greatest rival there, McGregor put in a terrific burst of speed right from the start – one which opened up such a gap that he did not need to worry about that final ten yards. He raced home, winning by more than half a second from Ilyichev, and a few moments later found himself at long last in the centre of the rostrum, receiving his Gold Medal.

The target was achieved. McGregor was 22, almost a veteran in the young world of swimming. Many expected him to retire. But he still had one further goal. He had not forgotten Tokyo, and he wanted to reverse that finish by beating Schollander.

He achieved his ambition at the little American town of Santa Clara. Though small, Santa Clara has produced more American Olympic swimmers than any other town, and winning there, under the noses of top class swimmers, was the greatest victory of Bobby McGregor's career. He said so – while he was still panting from the effort of beating Schollander by a fifth of a second!

Sir Alf Ramsey (centre) with Norman Hunter and Bobby Charlton

ALF RAMSEY

'WE want Alf!' was the shout. 'We want Alf!'

It came at the greatest moment in England's soccer history – that summer afternoon at Wembley in 1966 when England beat West Germany in the Final of the World Cup. And in response to the shout, the manager who had become known as 'the quiet man of soccer' came out to join in the celebration. No man had greater right to be in the front row of that march of triumph.

It could be said that the England victory was the outcome of four years' hard work, for it was in 1962 that Alf Ramsey took on the job of England's team manager. But really the story begins much earlier; ten years earlier, when, as a player with Spurs, Alf learned the classic style of football which he passed on to the young England trainees.

Alf Ramsey played 32 times for England – including the match in which England lost to the 'babes' of world soccer, the United States. In August 1955 he became manager of Ipswich, then a struggling Third Division side. There was no money to spare for the purchase of high-placed players; out of other clubs' rejects, Ramsey built a side which seven years later won the League Championship. So when the Football Association set out to find a man to lead England to World Cup victory, Alf Ramsey was an obvious choice. What he had to do was stake his reputation by picking an England squad of youngsters who would reach their peak in four years' time. Only masterly judgment could do that.

And it was masterly judgment that he showed. Gradually, as he introduced his picked men into the England team, he got the results he wanted. He won the right to keep his men together for longer training periods than ever before, so that they learned to play as a team, instead of as eleven stars unfamiliar with each other's styles. He was often tough on his players, but always scrupulously fair. He could lead – but he could also see the point of view of the men receiving his orders. The job of making a world-beating team was a mixture of planning, coaxing, begging, bullying, flattering, and teaching.

As every soccer enthusiast knows, it worked. Every move of that final against West Germany is well known, from the dozens of times it has been shown on television.

But it was not until 1970 that most people realized just what a triumph it had been. For by failing to win the Cup again, England – and Ramsey – revealed just how much skill, effort, and determination had been needed in 1966.

GORDON RICHARDS

In the late autumn of 1970 Sir Gordon Richards quietly gave up training racehorses. The sale of stables and equipment attracted little attention outside racing circles – but 16 years earlier his retirement as a jockey was a front page story in every newspaper.

It was in 1918 that a 4 foot 10 inch lad of 14 went along to a racing stable and asked for a job. His fellow stable-lads nicknamed him 'Moppy' because of his huge bush of hair. By 1925 he was Britain's champion jockey, and from then until 1953 there were only three years in which he did not win the championship – a record which is unlikely ever to be equalled. Altogether he rode 4,870 winners. Of the five Classic races, he won the 2,000 Guineas three times, the 1,000 Guineas also three times, the Oaks twice, and the St. Leger five times. The strange thing was that right up to 1953, the year before his retirement, he had never managed to win the greatest of them all – the Derby.

In 1953 he was 50. He had just received his knighthood – the first jockey ever to receive this honour. Could this be the year?

Certainly the crowds thought so, for his colt, Pinza, had been backed down to 5–1 joint favourite. But the Derby is a hard race to forecast, and as the runners thundered round the course, Pinza was only moderately placed.

Then, suddenly, Gordon Richards spotted an open space close in to the rails. He urged Pinza forward, moving up steadily from seventh to second place.

The crowd yelled him on. Ahead of him he could see his old rival Charlie Smirke on Shikampur – and beyond was the winning post!

And suddenly he was past – racing for the post, to complete a record of having won every major race in British flat racing!

ABEBE BIKILA

Just before the Tokyo Olympic Games of 1964, the hot favourite for the marathon was taken to hospital and had his appendix removed. For Abebe Bikila it was the most disappointing day in his life. Running barefoot, this soldier of the Royal Ethiopian Life Guard had won the marathon in 1960, and was determined to be the first man to win it twice.

When he arrived in Tokyo he was naturally no longer fancied as the winner. What man could cover 26 miles only five weeks after an operation – especially faced with such opposition as Australia's great Ron Clarke, Britain's Basil Heatley and Brian Kilby, and the Irishman Hogan?

When the race began, for the first hour the lead was held jointly by Hogan, Clarke, and Abebe, with all the attention along the route focussed on the magnificent figure of Clarke, legs jumping like pistons, seemingly immune to weariness.

But appearances were deceptive. Clarke *was* tiring, and tiring fast. He and Hogan dropped back, and by the half-way mark Abebe was well ahead.

Mile by mile, Abebe increased his lead still further, and when he entered the stadium, no other runner was in sight. Easily, steadily, he ran to the finish in the amazing time of 2 hours, 12 minutes, 11.2 seconds, with still enough strength left to turn and bow to the crowd, as composed as if he was walking to the start mark!

It was more than four minutes later that Basil Heatley

raced past two Japanese runners to take second place, and Brian Kilby finished fourth.

Abebe's success was not only a triumph for a country little noted in sport – but also for the surgeons!

TOMMY SIMPSON

ON the steep slope of Mount Ventoux in southern France a few years ago, Britain's greatest cyclist, Tommy Simpson, fell from his saddle and died – of exhaustion. It was a sad end to what had been a brilliant career, one dedicated not only to personal success, but also to the great ambition of being able to lead a strong British team in world class events abroad.

Tommy Simpson was 19 when he won his first national title as an amateur. He went on to international successes, and then turned professional, with steadily increasing triumph in road races on the continent. By 1964 he could outride and outstay almost any man in the world, and it was unusual for him to be outside the first six places in any international event. Even a crash in the 1965 Tour de France which nearly cost him an arm failed to halt his climb to the top, for only two months afterwards he finally carried off the World Road Race Championship. Cycling, which for years had been relegated to small corner paragraphs in British newspapers, hit the headlines again, and Tommy Simpson was voted Sportsman of the Year. The following year was another successful one, though again he crashed in the Tour de France, this time colliding with a motor cycle.

The Tour de France now became his greatest ambition. At 29, he knew he would have to win it soon, or the chance would pass him forever.

So in 1967 he tackled the race with even greater determination – determination which drove him to use booster stimulants which resulted in him passing the limit of physical endurance without realizing it and so causing him to collapse just two miles from the summit of the vicious 6,200 feet climb up Mount Ventoux. At the time, he was doing well; after 12 stages of the race he was among the eight leaders.

He had had five years at the top, earning – it was said – about £40,000 a year from cycling. It seems a lot to take out of a sport. But in terms of the encouragement he gave to British cycling, perhaps it could be said that he put even more in than he took out.

VLADIMIR KUTS

In the tradition of the armed forces all the world over, the Chief Petty Officer of the Russian Navy took the easiest method of picking his team. 'I want six volunteers,' he said. 'You, and you, and you – and you, and you, and you.'

That was how Vladimir Kuts found himself taking part in an annual 3,000 metres cross-country race to celebrate the anniversary of the end of the war in Europe.

To his surprise, he did quite well, and was retained in his ship's team for the next two years. He had always believed that if a thing was worth doing, it was worth doing well, so in 1951 before the race he put in a spell of really intensive training under some of Russia's leading coaches.

This time he won.

After that, he no longer needed to be picked as a 'volunteer'. He had set himself a target, to be an even better runner than the great Czechoslovak, Emil Zatopek. He achieved this when he beat Zatopek in the European Championships of 1954. But the race which made Kuts a man to be remembered in Britain was his 5,000 metres battle against Chris Chataway at the White City in London.

It was a personal duel between two dedicated men. For days in advance the newspapers had highlighted the rivalry between them. On the day of the race itself, the floodlit White City, so often half empty for even the biggest athletics match, was crammed with 40,000 people, and millions more watched on TV.

Lap after lap the two men pounded along side by side, Kuts in a red running vest, and Chataway with hair that almost matched it. Occasionally one of them would open up a slight gap, only to lose it again within seconds. The speed was terrific for a race of this distance. Experts glanced at their stopwatches, excitedly checking lap times against those of the existing world record. The final lap began, and a spotlight from the stands picked out the two rivals. Thousands of roaring spectators leaped to their feet. It was a British crowd but they were cheering both men. Into the last turn they came, shoulder to shoulder. Chataway moved up a fraction. Kuts held off his challenge. But then the Russian made a fatal mistake. He thought the finish was well down the straight, and he believed that Chataway was too exhausted to hold on. Chataway made another burst which took him inches in front, and breasted the tape, which was near the start of the straight, in a world record of 13 minutes 51.6 seconds.

Though Kuts went on to win Gold Medals for the 5,000 and 10,000 metres, and later set another world record himself for 5,000 metres, years later when he retired and was asked whether there was anything else he would have liked from athletics, he said, 'Just one more race like that against Chataway!'

SONJA HENIE

THE first time the world heard about Sonja Henie was in 1927. It was then, at the age of only 13, that she won the World Figure Skating Championship for Women. But in her native Norway she was already famous.

She had begun skating soon after her sixth birthday, and soon became the youngest girl ever to win the Norwegian Championship. She won the European title eight times in a row, but even more amazing, her World Championship in 1927 was the first of *ten* consecutive victories. That in itself is a world record – and it would no doubt have become an even more impressive one if she had not turned professional in 1936 and thus been unable to compete in the following years.

To add to her Norwegian, European, and World Championships Sonja also won a stream of Gold Medals in the Winter Olympics of 1928, 1932, and 1936.

It was determination which had started her on her skating career – a determination which had carried her past the opposition from her parents. But by the time she was twenty it had all become so easy that determination was no longer needed. When somebody asked her how she managed to do some of her most difficult figures, she replied, 'They may *look* difficult, but I find them easy. You see, a great wave of happiness seems to come over me every time I glide out on the ice.'

By 1936, Sonja Henie had achieved everything possible for an amateur skater, and she now turned her attention to making skating secure her future. She was 22, blonde, attractive – and the Hollywood film industry was at its height. Norway could offer her success, but not money, so she moved to the United States, where the crowds would pay highly to see her, and where the film offers soon began to come in. She starred in several big colour 'spectaculars' in which her skating dazzled the audiences – and she invested her earnings wisely. In 1968 she was listed as one of the ten richest women in the world.

She also received a title from her king – in recognition of her services to Norwegian sport.

FREDDIE MILLS

The story of Freddie Mills is that of a boxer whose career was spoiled by trying to do too much.

A whirling tornado of punches, sometimes so fast that the boxing commentators had difficulty in describing what was happening, plus a complete disregard of the blows coming back at him – that is the way Freddie Mills is remembered; perhaps it is *why* he is remembered. For traditionally, if perhaps a little unfairly, British heavyweight boxers have been regarded as defensive fighters. Freddie was never like that.

He was 16 when he won his first professional fight, by a knockout. Six years later, in 1942, after 74 professional bouts, he beat the veteran Len Harvey for the British and Empire Light-heavyweight titles. It was then that the frustration began. There is plenty of honour in winning Light-heavyweight titles, but it is the Heavyweight Championship fights that draw the crowds and bring in the big money. Mills's natural weight was 12 stone 7 pounds – too light for the Heavyweight division. In 1944, in spite of this, he took his chance and challenged Jack London for the Empire Heavyweight title. To his bitter disappointment he was outpointed, and so he reluctantly moved back into the 'Light-heavies' to fight for the World title against America's Gus Lesnevich.

This was a tremendous struggle between two hard-attacking boxers. Four seconds from the end of the 10th round, the referee stepped in and awarded the fight to Lesnevich. But though Mills had been on the canvas four times, it was the American who showed the most damage.

Mills made his second attempt to turn heavyweight, only to be beaten in six rounds by the American, Joe Baksi, and outpointed by Britain's Bruce Woodcock. So back he went again to the light-heavies, for a further title fight against Lesnevich.

This took place on 26th July, 1948, and the crowd saw a very different Mills. Instead of the usual barrage of punches and the casual defence, Freddie showed a cool, calm approach to the fight. He selected his opportunities, weaving and tacking with clever footwork to get in through the American's guard. Lesnevich, unprepared for this change of style, took too long to adjust himself and allowed Mills to build up a big points lead. The fight went to the full 15 rounds, and Freddie Mills came out of it as World Light-heavyweight Champion.

If he had been content with this, all would have been well. But once again success tempted him into the heavy-weights, with the same disastrous result as before. He took such a beating from Bruce Woodcock in a heavy-weight bout that he was in no condition to defend his world title, and lost it at the first challenge. There can be no doubt that if he had stuck to what he did well, his career would have been twice as successful.

W. G. GRACE

W. G. GRACE belongs to a very small group of sportsmen whose names have become household words. Described as 'The Grand Old Man of English Cricket', W.G. *looked* it. His massive beard gave him a look of confidence – or disguised his nervousness – at the worst moments in his career.

Not that there were many. And it was a very long career. When he entered cricket, it was a club game; when he retired, the County Championship and the Tests had made it the nation's second sport. Born in 1848, he was playing for Gloucestershire in his early teens; he took part in some of the earliest Tests against Australia, and was sixty when he retired after scoring 54,896 runs at an average of 39.55.

His batting figures give some idea of the man, for when he was young, the wickets were biased in favour of the bowlers. Modern turf had not been developed, nor had modern multi-blade mowers. Early photographs of cricket pitches show that the surface of the pitch was as rough as most outfields are today. On this kind of wicket the batsman needed great skill and lightning reflexes, because it was almost impossible to tell in advance what line the ball would take as it came off the pitch. To succeed, a batsman had to be able to score equally well with every type of stroke – and it was in this that W. G. Grace excelled. In spite of the perils of batting on rough wickets, he never scored 'a pair of spectacles' – a double duck – in his life!

Even in those days of low scores, he made 344 for

M.C.C. against Kent in 1876, an individual record that stood for 19 years. At the age of 47, in 1895, he became the first cricketer to score 1,000 runs in the month of May. He described this as 'the crowning point of my career'. Opposing teams did not know whether to fear him more as a batsman or as a bowler. He was a brilliant fielder to his own bowling. He generally fielded at point, but when bowling he would follow up and move across to act as an extra mid-off. He bowled slow medium leg-breaks, which were very effective on those unpredictable wickets.

Before he died, in 1915, W.G. had seen cricket change from a very primitive game to what it is today. But he would certainly not have approved of today's tactics of defensive play. The greatest tonic modern cricket could have would be the return of W.G. – striding out into the doldrums of a defensive game to open it up with the full power of his shoulders!

JOHN CHARLES

Most top sportsmen like to end their careers while they are still at the top. John Charles was an exception.

Leeds United took him on in 1948, when he was 16. It was a wise decision, for by the time this tall, lanky Welsh boy was 18 he had a regular place at centre-forward, and had won the first of his caps for Wales. In the mid-nineteen-fifties it looked as though he would spend his whole playing career with Leeds. The club's tactics were built round Big John's goal-making and goal-scoring, and so it came as a shock to Leeds supporters when in April 1957 he was transferred to the Italian club Juventus for a fee of at least £65,000, possibly £10,000 more.

A year later, John Charles was top scorer in the Italian League, with 27 goals – and Juventus had won the Championship. They won it again, and the fans named him King John – 'the greatest man in football'.

John Charles was never the greatest man in football, but his five years in Italy brought excitement and attacking play into a League which had settled into a dreary pattern of defensive football.

It was Leeds who brought John Charles home again; not the triumphant Leeds of earlier years, but a club now in the Second Division and struggling to get back into senior soccer. They paid £53,000 for him, but it was a bad investment. John Charles could not settle. In 11 games, he scored only three goals. His play looked tired and dispirited, and when Roma offered £70,000 to take him back to Italy, Leeds, not surprisingly, jumped at the offer.

Roma supporters who had read about John Charles's poor performances for Leeds were horrified. At his first game, many came expecting to boo him off the field. But they stayed to cheer as he scored and then set up two more goals for his team-mates. Once again John Charles was 'King John', with his name in the headlines almost every day.

But this time his stay in Italy was short – from November 1962 until the following August. He could not sustain his brilliant start. After a spell of poor form, his transfer value dropped by about £50,000. It is said that Cardiff City paid only £20,000 to bring him back to his native Wales for a final three seasons in league soccer. After 30 Welsh caps, and a total of transfer fees amounting to about £200,000, John Charles was finally given a free transfer in May 1966.

Many players who have been at the top cannot face the prospect of playing in minor soccer. But John Charles had learned enough about football *off* the field to be able to take on enthusiastically the dual job of player manager with Hereford United. And there, he was 'King John' again!

JIM PETERS

Some great sportsmen are remembered for their successes. Jim Peters is famous for one of the most gallant failures in sporting history – a failure that choked the cheers in 40,000 throats on a blisteringly hot day in Vancouver on 7th August, 1954. The event was the Commonwealth Games Marathon, and the excitement in the crowd was because they had heard so much beforehand about Britain's Jim Peters, 'the man who had revolutionized the marathon'.

His revolution was speed. Top marathon runners were quite content to jog along at a snail's pace mile after mile, confident that the less experienced men who had gone into the lead would run themselves out long before the finish. But Peters had copied the rigorous training methods of the 10,000 metres runners, applied them to the marathon, and by means of them already broken the world marathon record twice.

Sixteen men lined up at the start. It was the height of the Canadian summer, and the sun blazed down, creating a heat haze. On the roads the tar was melting. After only a few miles, many of the runners knew they had no chance of finishing the course in such killing heat. The field dwindled away until only eight men were left. The front man, far ahead of his rivals, was Jim Peters. The crowds lining the route were uncertain whether to cheer him or beg him to stop. For many miles the sweat dripped off him; then there was no more sweat. His body had dried out. His physical reserves were gone, only sheer determination kept him on his feet

– and the knowledge that the race was nearly run.

What Jim Peters had not reckoned with was the short steep gradient inside the tunnel to the stadium. His balance, which had been automatic for mile after mile, now failed him. From glaring sunshine he had gone into deep shade. Then, as he came out again into the stadium which the hot sun had turned into a gigantic frying pan, he swayed, his knees buckled, and he fell.

Even those with no knowledge of medicine could see that this was a man who had gone far beyond the normal limits. His body, looking almost shrivelled by the heat which had dried out all its moisture, was laboriously dragged along the ground. It took him nearly twelve minutes to cover half the distance from the stadium entrance to the finishing tape. He fell six times in all. Only when he pitched forward and lay motionless did Red Cross men run forward with a stretcher, to take the gallant near-winner away for seven hours in an oxygen tent.

There are still arguments over whether he should have been allowed to go on, or stopped even earlier. But those who argue are all agreed on one thing – that this was one of the most gallant runners of all time.

LEN HUTTON

In the summer of 1938 Sir Leonard Hutton played in his first Test against Australia, and crowned the series with an astonishing innings of 364 which lasted two and a half days and stood as a Test record until 1957–8 when Gary Sobers of the West Indies, facing a very weak Pakistan attack, slogged his way to 365 not out simply for the sake of beating it.

The Second World War wrecked some cricket careers, but not Hutton's. The only injury he suffered during the war was caused by an accident in a gymnasium. As a result of this, his left arm was inches shorter than his right. When he returned to cricket, the experts said he could not possibly regain his pre-war form with such a handicap. Hutton proved them wrong. By 1950 he had reached a peak of batting which made him the obvious choice as England's captain two years later. During his captaincy, which lasted for 23 Tests, England won 11, lost 4, and drew 8. Australia were beaten both in England and on their own soil, for the first time in a quarter of a century.

Len Hutton was not a calm, nerveless giant. For him every match was a battle which absorbed every last fraction of his thoughts and energy. Off the field his word was law. His players did not always find him an easy skipper to deal with, but if sometimes they felt they were being treated like children when they were off the field, they had to forgive him next day when his efforts on the field gave them the example and the encouragement to make England cricket's 'top dogs' for the first time in years.

Hundreds of later cricketers based their style on Hutton's batting. It was a defence which bowlers despaired of breaking, coupled with a cover drive of a quality which has seldom been seen before or since. But the crowd not only rose to their feet with applause for the fours which sneaked through gaps in the field; they also appreciated the oddities which lasted throughout Hutton's career. There was the old-fashioned, nineteenth-century way in which Hutton touched his cap between balls, and the stance between overs as he quietly sized up the field positions.

Hutton made thousands of people into cricket fans, just as Stanley Matthews brought soccer into the lives of many who had never cared for sport at all.

ROCKY MARCIANO

Rocky Marciano's record of 49 major fights without defeat is unequalled in heavyweight history, and almost impossible to beat.

Few people expected him to become World Heavyweight Champion in the first place. On 23rd September, 1952, in Philadelphia, he faced the wily old veteran, Jersey Joe Walcott. Walcott was 38, ten years older than Marciano, and though the younger man had beaten many top fighters on his way up, it soon looked as if at last he had met his match. Almost immediately Walcott caught him with a hook to the chin which put him down for a count of five. Walcott, with his years of experience, then kept him dazed and on the defensive, never letting up, scoring with punch after punch as the rounds went by.

In round 6, Marciano's head was cut. By round 13, his face was puffy and swollen, and he was so far behind on points that the only way he could win was by a knock-out.

Marciano did the only thing possible. He let himself appear even more dazed and exhausted than he really was – and not even Jersey Joe's experience warned him against the trap. When Walcott dropped his guard, Marciano's right snaked out, and at the count of ten he had become the first white World Heavyweight Champion since James Braddock lost the title 15 years earlier.

In a return fight eight months later, Marciano knocked out Walcott in the first round. He then went on to defend the title five times, and on all but one occasion he was the winner by a knockout.

In 1955 he fought for the last time, against Archie Moore. When Moore dropped him in the second round, it was only the second time in his career that he had been down on the canvas. The crowd were on their feet, unable to believe that at long last his incredible record was ending.

They need not have worried.

Marciano was on his feet again well within the count of ten. He went on to knock out Moore in the ninth round, and retire from the ring as undefeated champion.

MAUREEN CONNOLLY

WHEN a 16-year-old girl became the United States Women's Tennis Champion the game, which had been losing its hold in American schools and colleges, was suddenly given a new lease of life. And in 1952, when she was just 17, Americans flocked to Britain to see Maureen Connolly at Wimbledon.

Her path to the quarter finals was easy, as everyone expected. But then came bad news – she had shoulder trouble. A rumour spread round the courts that she was going to withdraw.

But somehow the girl who had become known as Little Mo struggled on, to stand one set all against a home player she would normally have beaten with the loss of hardly a game. Then, in the third set, clearly in great discomfort, she began to trail. A few of her supporters, unable to watch their champion in agony, left the court.

They missed a fighting recovery which gave Maureen the match, and also the confidence to battle on through her semi-final to a final against Louise Brough, whom she beat 7–5, 6–3.

Little Mo was now undisputed world champion – at 17. The following year, as well as beating Doris Hart 8–6, 7–5 in the Wimbledon final, she won the Australian, French, and American Championships to complete the 'big four'. Then in 1954 she won the Wimbledon title yet again, beating Louise Brough 6–2, 7–5, to round off a grand total of three American and two French titles, and three at Wimbledon.

There seemed no reason why Little Mo should not
continue to dominate the world's top tennis courts for
another ten years. But then, while out riding, Maureen
took a bad fall, and broke her leg. She never returned to
tennis.

DIXIE DEAN

IN 1927 George Camsell of Middlesbrough set a Football League scoring record of 59 goals. It was an amazing achievement, and nobody thought it could ever be beaten.

Nobody, that is, except Everton's Dixie Dean. He was already becoming a legend on Merseyside, and was described as England's greatest centre-forward. In the 1927–28 season he was as successful as in the past, and by mid April Everton were almost certain champions of the First Division, thanks to his 50 goals. But 50 is a long way short of 59, and Everton had only three games left.

Most men would have left it, and tried again next season. But not Dixie Dean. In the first of the three games he scored four times! In the second, he got another three!

That left him three goals to get for a record – but only one single game left! The question whether he could get them was the headline story in every newspaper on the Saturday that Everton came out at Goodison Park to play Arsenal. Sixty thousand people packed into the ground – and after two minutes a great roar went up.

Dixie Dean had scored!

Arsenal equalized, and the effect was to galvanize Dean into a spell of play that was almost unbelievable. He brought the Everton forwards into attack after attack – and suddenly Everton were in front again. And it was Dixie Dean who had scored, to equal Camsell's record.

But at half time, with only another 45 minutes' play left in the 1927–8 season, the one goal needed must have seemed to him more than he could hope for. And in the second half, when the crowd were shouting 'Give it to Dixie!' every time the ball reached an Everton player, the 45 minutes ebbed away fast. Arsenal's defence stood firm.

Then, with eight minutes to go, there came a swift Everton attack down the left wing. The winger halted the ball just short of the line, glanced across the field – and there was Dixie Dean racing into the penalty area.

The ball came to him high and hard. He leaped high above the other heads which shot up towards it – and deflected it hard into the back of the net!

Dixie Dean played on until 1939, broke other records, and created a Merseyside legend. But that 60 goal record stands out above all the rest.

HAROLD LARWOOD

On 18th January, 1933, an angry telegram was sent by the Australian Cricket Board of Control to the M.C.C. It claimed that body-line bowling was endangering batsmen and causing intensely bitter feelings between players.

The telegram was sent on the fifth day of the Third Test at Adelaide. England had won the First, and lost the Second. The M.C.C.'s reply was an offer to cancel the tour. It was not accepted, and England went on to win the Third, Fourth, and Fifth Tests.

The man all the fuss was about was one of the unforgettable men in cricket, Harold Larwood, a tough Nottinghamshire miner who came up from the pits to play for his county in 1924. He developed what the M.C.C. described as 'leg-theory' bowling – he bowled fast on the leg side, with the field so placed that the batsman, defending, was likely to put up a catch.

After a brief experience of this technique, the Australians had a different name for it! Several, in fact, of which 'body-line' was the most polite. They maintained that Larwood was actually bowling not at the wicket, but at the batsman.

The rights and wrongs of the matter were hotly argued. England put their case by means of diagrams and theories. The Australians argued theirs, during the Third Test, by producing two bruised and angry batsmen – Oldfield, who retired with an injured head, and Woodfall, who had a series of dark, swollen lumps round his waistline.

But Harold Larwood bowled on, ignoring the argument. One of the calmest and most detached descriptions of his bowling (it did not come from Oldfield or Woodfall!) was, 'He gets great pace off the ground, probably because he has a perfect run-up to the wicket, and at times he makes the ball come back so much that he is almost unplayable.'

Harold Larwood was certainly unplayable that season in Australia, for in the five Tests he took 33 wickets, and topped the bowling averages. But the effort of bowling leg-theory was tremendous; by the end of the tour the mental and physical strain had cut his speed, and he never reached Test standard again. When he retired a few years later, he emigrated to Australia. Australians had forgiven him. Thirty years afterwards, he was still signing autograph books!

SPIRIDON LOUES

WHEN the Olympic games were revived in 1896 the Greeks were no longer the athletes they had been two thousand years earlier. Britain, France, the United States and Germany sent men who had been brought up in the new athletic tradition of the 19th century; Greece's athletic tradition had died in A.D. 393 when the original Games came to an end.

And so there was a monotonous succession of overseas victories. The Greek crowd in the stands groaned with every foreign success. What they needed was a man like Pheidippides, who had won the original marathon by running 26 miles to carry the news of a victory.

The organizers of the modern Olympics had instituted the Marathon in his memory, and long distance runners had come to Athens from all over the world to take part. But the Greeks themselves were hardly interested. They had no long distance runners, and so they hardly bothered to watch the start.

But they were, after all, destined to have a hero!

Among the entrants was a young Greek called Spiridon Loues. This was an unknown name in athletics – he was simply a hardy shepherd boy whose training had been the work of rounding up his sheep in the rough, hilly country to the north of Athens.

As was expected, the lead in the race was shared among Frenchmen, Americans, and Australians. The finish was to be in the stadium, after an exhausting three hours of plodding over rough roads and mountain paths. To make matters worse, the circuit had been made even more gruelling by the clouds of dust thrown up by the hooves of the Greek cavalry escort riding ahead.

As the time of the finish drew near, many Greeks left the stands and went home. What was the use of waiting? News had reached them that Australia's E. H. Flack was leading, with an American lying second.

Then, suddenly, the leader appeared in the entrance to the stadium – and it was not Flack! It was the small and slender figure of Spiridon Loues, fighting his way gallantly towards the finishing line. As he ran on, a great burst of cheering broke from ten thousand throats. The tall figures of two Greek princes took their places beside Loues, and escorted him to the finish!

GILLIAN SHEEN

British sports fans, waiting anxiously for news from the Melbourne Olympics in 1956, let out a cheer when it was learned Gillian Sheen had won a Gold Medal. Hooray – but what was it for?

Fencing was not a major British sport. Few people had ever seen it take place. It was something normally left to Frenchmen and Hungarians.

So who was this mysterious Gillian Sheen, bless her?

She was, in fact, a ginger haired dentist with a mischievous smile and an extraordinary ability with the foil, that light fencing weapon which demands tremendous concentration, speed, and reaction. She had been National Schoolgirl Champion, National Junior Champion, and then a British international. But fencing, now so popular, was then a sport which seldom found its way into the newspapers. She became British Champion, and most people did not know. And she arrived in Melbourne as a complete unknown.

The scene was set. Competitors are drawn in pools of six or eight, and every competitor fences against every other. In the first round pool, to the consternation of the continentals, Gillian was the winner. She sailed through the second round. And then came the final, and she found herself in a fence-off to decide who would win the Gold Medal. Her opponent was Olga Orban of Rumania, against whom she had lost only a few hours earlier!

The Rumanians rubbed their hands together,

confident of victory. But to their surprise, Gillian Sheen ran up a 3–1 lead over the Rumanian girl. Her team-mates recalled later how they had to turn away; the tension was too much. One more hit – and Gillian would be Olympic Champion!

But it was Olga Orban who scored next.

Once again the two fencers crossed foils, and the high speed bout was on again, with lightning thrusts and parries, watched with bated breath by the team-mates of both girls.

And then suddenly the light of the electric judging gear flashed. Gillian Sheen had scored the vital hit. The Gold Medal was hers.

But the medal was less important than the effect it had. Suddenly British fencing was 'on the map'. Instead of being a forgotten sport, it was one with popular appeal.

HERB ELLIOTT

AT the age of 24, Herb Elliott retired from international athletics after four years at the top during which he had run no fewer than 17 sub-four-minute miles. His first was in Melbourne in 1958. What had started him off was the sight of Russia's Vladimir Kuts in action at the Melbourne Olympics two years earlier, and a meeting with Percy Cerutty, a ruthless trainer of champions.

Cerutty saw in Elliott a magnificent physique of the kind possessed by so many Australians thanks to their outdoor life. He also saw someone completely without any of the iron discipline needed to become a world champion. Elliott ran because he liked it – not for records and titles.

Cerutty changed all that. In the depths of the Australian dead season in athletics, when other runners were relaxing, Cerutty had Elliott in training throughout the week, before and after work. On Saturdays Cerutty took him 60 miles out of Melbourne, and on lonely sand dunes would make him start off with a fourteen mile trot. Every mile on sand is worth two anywhere else for exhaustion. The fourteen miles had to end with a sprint finish.

They also discussed every step of this training. They discussed the split second at which Elliott reached the threshold of pain – the point at which effort became unbearable – and by planning changes in the training, moved the threshold farther and farther away. This, after all, is the purpose of almost all training – to postpone exhaustion.

Elliott's exhaustion was postponed to the point at which he could still summon up a sprint after a long hard race. His first sub-four-minute mile was 3 minutes 59.9 seconds, but from this he went on to a mile in Dublin at 3 minutes 54.5, a world record. There were also two world records for the 1,500 metres, the second of them at the Rome Olympics of 1960.

But the partnership could not last. Elliott went to Cambridge University. His career began to count more than records. And there was no Cerutty to discuss plans, and drive him on. So Elliott went back to running for pleasure.

LAURIE DOHERTY

THE south-east entrance to Wimbledon is known as 'The Doherty Gate', in memory of Laurie Doherty and his brother Reggie, who between them created Wimbledon's claim to be the top tournament in international tennis.

Tennis in the eighteen-nineties was very much a polite game of patball, in which trying hard was considered bad manners. Into this the Dohertys introduced a devastating accuracy of strokes, particularly off the backhand – something which until then had been neglected by the majority of players. Laurie Doherty brought new techniques in volleying and smashing, plus an ability to leap across the court at tremendous speed to return a fast service.

When these two appeared at Wimbledon, the crowds came too. Reggie won the singles from 1897 to 1900, then Laurie won them from 1902 to 1906. Together they won the doubles in every year but one from 1897 to 1905.

In the Davis Cup, Laurie played twelve times in the Challenge round without being beaten, and ensured that Britain won the Cup in 1903 and retained it to 1906.

During their years of domination, it became the ambition of every overseas player to go to Wimbledon and try to beat them. The more they failed, the more they came back again. Thanks to them both, but particularly to Laurie the unbeatable, Wimbledon became established as the final goal of every top tennis player in the world. And so, when the crowds pour in each summer, there are always a few old-timers who halt at the south-east gate, look up, and remember to say thank you.

BEN HOGAN

Few men reach the top in sport twice. But Ben Hogan was an exception.

Born in Texas in 1912, he became a professional golfer when he was 17. It was a struggle to reach the top, one which took him many years, but by 1945 he had become the biggest money-winner in American tournaments, which he remained for the next two years. He was the American Professional Champion in 1946, 1947, and 1948, and American Open Champion in 1948.

He could go no higher than this. He was recognized everywhere as the world's Number 1.

Then, early in 1949 he and his wife were critically injured in a car smash. For hours doctors fought to save their lives. 'One thing's certain,' they said, 'Ben Hogan will never be able to play professional golf again.'

The only person who was not convinced of this was Ben himself. When he began a gentle work-out over a putting course during his convalescence, doctors and nurses pitied him. He looked nothing more than the wreck of a man who had once been an expert. A year later, after he had returned to big tournament play and entered the United States Open Championship once again, nobody believed he had the remotest chance of winning. But he did!

Incredibly, Hogan was back at the top. He could scarcely believe his own success. 'It doesn't matter what happens now,' he gasped to reporters. 'Nothing can ever equal this. It's the greatest moment in my life.'

Perhaps he was right – in terms of his own personal feelings. But in terms of success, he had as much still ahead of him as all that had gone before. Ryder Cup Captain, Golfer of the Year four times, winner of the British Open Championship in 1953 at his only attempt, he was finally voted the Greatest Professional Golfer of all Time.

JIMMY GREAVES

To be a star player for Chelsea, Spurs, and then West Ham, to appear for England more than fifty times, yet to be passed over for England's World Cup squad in 1966 and 1970 has been the curious fate of Jimmy Greaves, a player who will still be discussed as one of soccer's curiosities long after he has retired from the game.

Aged 17, he signed professional forms for Chelsea in 1957, and it was not long before the club discovered the £10 signing on fee had been well spent. In the four years he spent with them he scored 124 of their 334 goals! In his final season with them he set a club individual record of 41 goals, and after his last game for the club, in which he scored all four of their goals in a 4-3 win over Nottingham Forest, he was chaired off the field.

So began what Jimmy Greaves expected to be a great adventure. He was transferred to the Italian club, Milan, for a fee of £80,000. Regarded as the great new discovery in English football, he was going to the 'glamour' club of European soccer.

Seldom before or since can a soccer star's excitement and enthusiasm have been turned so rapidly into utter despair and disillusionment. Greaves's career with Milan was short and stormy. There were blazing arguments with officials, team-mates, and opponents – and he went right off form. The marksmanship which had been internationally famous was no longer perfect. Team members who had become his enemies no longer gave him the passes on which he relied.

The man who took him out of the toughest spot in his life was Spur's manager Billy Nicholson, who paid a transfer fee of £99,999, the largest sum paid until then by any English club. Spurs supporters thought Nicholson was crazy! But Greaves promptly proved he was not, by scoring three goals in his first game for them.

Since then there have been good seasons and bad, and a change of team style at Spurs meant letting him go to West Ham. He remains an unpredictable player, terrible when out of form, but able, on a good day, to conjure up classic goals which set the terraces ablaze.

JUAN FANGIO

'EL CHUECO' was what they called Juan Manuel Fangio in his home town in Argentina, but it was not meant as a compliment. In English it meant 'Bandy Legs'.

He was one of six children; in the nineteen-twenties there was not much money about, and Juan was expected to become a plasterer like his father or be forced to earn his living in the potato fields. But El Chueco had other ideas. Outside the town there was a dusty track of mud on which young drivers raced 'hotrods' built from bits of cars salvaged from scrap heaps. Juan joined them – but as second pit mechanic, almost unpaid, to the least successful of the local drivers.

He was 25 before he got his first chance to drive in a race. This was in a borrowed car, but meanwhile, out of his small pay as a mechanic, he had been buying parts and building a car of his own. It took him two years, and in its first race it came in third – with Juan at the wheel.

For the first time he heard the crowds cheering *him*!

From that point on there was no turning back. In 1940, driving a new car provided by Chevrolet, he drove in a tremendous long distance race, the Gran Premio del Norte. It was a road race, over boulder-strewn surfaces all the way from Buenos Aires to Peru and back, with climbs to 15,000 feet. He finished the 6,000 miles in 13 days – and won.

In a similar race his car skidded through a flimsy

barrier on a hairpin bend, and careered down a mountainside. His co-driver was killed, and Juan, recovering in hospital, vowed never to try mountain racing again. Instead, he left for Europe with a $1\frac{1}{2}$ litre Maserati, and won six races in his first season. In 1950, driving an Alfa-Romeo, he finished second in the World Championship. A year later he become World Champion, and won the title twice more, for Mercedes.

There were more crashes. In 1952 at Monza in Italy his car spun off the track, and he spent months with his neck in plaster. Later the great Le Mans disaster, when he had to weave his way at top speed through a litter of smashed cars, warned him that he, like a cat, had only nine lives, and was using them up too fast. He retired in 1958 while still at the top, with the fortune made from racing now well invested in a business in Argentina.

The business, of course, is the building of racing cars!

ROGER BANNISTER

THEY cheered him on, but even while they cheered, they knew he had failed. The young medical student, gasping his way down the last few yards of the home straight, no longer had any hope of being the first man in the world to run a mile in under four minutes.

As he broke the tape, in four minutes and two seconds, his friends congratulated him on a magnificent run – but already they were wondering if, while Roger Bannister was failing, one of his rivals might have picked the same day to run, and succeeded.

The rivals were Wes Santee, in America, and John Landy, in Australia. They were all after the same elusive target.

But Bannister was undeterred by failure. He did not run just to win fame and set up athletics records; he ran because as a medical student he was making a serious study of just what stress and strain the human body could take. For years, people had bet that the four minute barrier could never be broken. He was determined to prove them wrong.

It was on a gloomy, damp evening in Oxford that he tried again. With his colleagues Chris Chataway and Chris Brasher to help as pacemakers, he did it at last – a brilliant mile in 3 minutes 59.4 seconds. The record stood for forty days.

Then, in Finland, on a track that experts considered the finest in the world, the Australian, John Landy, cut the new record down by more than a second.

And now the two men waited for a chance to race against one another. Every follower of athletics waited, too. The chance came quickly, in the Commonwealth Games of 1954, at Vancouver. South of the border, in the United States, Wes Santee is said to have sent a personal telegram to the President, asking that the United States rejoin the British Empire after nearly 200 years – so that he could compete!

It was hot. Landy, always a pacemaker, streaked ahead, leading Bannister by ten yards. The tension in the crowd began to burst out, in a growing roar of encouragement as it was realized that a four minute mile was almost a certainty. At the bell, Landy's time was 2 minutes 58.3 – but now Bannister was closing the gap. Suddenly Landy, realizing his danger, put on a spurt.

Bannister let him reopen the gap. Not until they came into the home straight did he summon up a magnificent finishing burst that carried him past.

The time was just outside Landy's record, but the race became known as 'The Mile of the Century' – for it was the first contest between men who had beaten the barrier.

FOXHUNTER

In the final of any big show jumping competition there is always a hushed silence among the spectators. But to most of the crowd, though horses are skilful, well-trained, and able to show their breeding, they are certainly not human.

One man who learned to disagree was Colonel Harry Llewellyn. His amazing partnership with Foxhunter taught him that perhaps horses *are* human after all.

The day he made the discovery was the final day of the Helsinki Olympics. On their partnership depended Britain's last chance of a Gold Medal – and Foxhunter was jumping badly. Llewellyn was puzzled. The horse was clearly unwell, and dropped more than 16 points in the early stages. Britain's other entries also did badly.

As Llewellyn came out on Foxhunter for the afternoon round, it looked as though another disastrous performance was coming, one which would finally wreck all Britain's hopes. Foxhunter moved slowly, nervously, as if unwilling to attempt the round at all. The crowd was silent. Lewellyn coaxed Foxhunter to the start.

For a few seconds the horse stood absolutely still, except for the muscles of his mighty shoulders, which quivered with tension. It was as if he knew what kind of performance would be needed from him, and was fighting for the courage and strength to give it.

Then he began to move.

He gave a mighty leap to clear the first jump – and there was a loud knock as one hind hoof rapped the bar.

It shuddered – and so did British supporters! But the bar stayed in place.

Foxhunter ran on to the next jump, clearing it smoothly and easily, then on to the next, and the next, surmounting each with magnificent leaps that left the watchers breathless with suspense. Foreign riders who had hoped to win the Gold Medal themselves stared in amazement, unable to believe that a horse could stage such a brilliant recovery. After each jump, wild cheering broke out in the stands.

Then, with a final jump, Foxhunter completed a clear round.

The cheering was redoubled. Officials ran out to award the Gold Medal to Britain.

Did Foxhunter realize what he had done? Only Foxhunter knew – and perhaps Colonel Llewellyn, the man on his back at that astonishing moment when the great horse pulled himself together and clearly became conscious of how much depended on him alone.

Francis Lee (centre) with Bob McNab and Tommy Wright

FRANCIS LEE

In 1967 Manchester City took on Francis Lee from Bolton Wanderers, and they have been congratulating themselves on their good judgment ever since.

He had already showed himself to be one of football's startling characters. In his first match for Bolton he scored an impressive goal, but while still glowing with the triumph of this, he had his name taken by the referee!

For City, in 1970, he scored a goal from the penalty spot in teeming rain in Vienna, to give them a 2–1 victory over Gornik Zabrze of Poland in the final of the European Cup Winners' Cup. The medal for this joined an impressive handful already gained during his few years with the club – a League Championship Medal, an F.A. Cup Winners' Medal, and a League Cup Winners' Medal.

Essentially a striker, depending on support from behind for his goalscoring, he was City's top scorer in

League matches in 1969–70, with 13 goals, and there were high hopes of equal success when he went to Mexico for the World Cup in the following summer. Lack of support prevented him from playing at his best, but he rapidly showed that this had not affected his form when the 1970–71 League season began.

Lee's importance in northern football is that after years in which Manchester City had been totally overshadowed by Manchester United, he provided much of the excitement and the success which restored City to prominence.

SONNY RAMADHIN

THERE is a song about it, and people still refer to it as the 'Feast of Ramadhin and Valentine's Day'. The match is remembered as the greatest in West Indian cricket history – it was the Second Test at Lord's. England had won the First by a comfortable margin of 202 runs, but when the Second began, the West Indies made a determined start, scoring 326 by the morning of the second day.

It was when England came out to reply that the threat of Sonny Ramadhin and his partner Valentine made itself felt for the first time. Ramadhin's bowling baffled even the most experienced batsmen. Most of the time he sent down off-spinners, but every so often, without any visible change of action, he'd turn the ball the opposite way and leave the batsman swatting wildly at thin air. Out went Hutton. Edrich and Washbrook, two equally experienced batsmen, could do nothing but defend desperately. At the lunch break, England supporters had every justification in looking gloomy. The gloom spread rapidly afterwards, when Washbrook was out, followed by a stream of other batsmen. Only Edrich was able to hold off the onslaught. Between them, Ramadhin and Valentine shared 9 wickets – and nobody could blame the pitch, for when the West Indies batted again they were able to run up such a mighty score that they declared, and set England the task of batting for eleven hours to avoid defeat – or scoring 600 to win!

By now, to the England players, Ramadhin and Valentine looked almost superhuman. They had destroyed the morale of the batsmen, and so each man came out already doubting his ability to survive.

And they did not survive.

The crowd was sharply divided. England supporters sat in breathless silence – but here and there were clusters of West Indians, shouting with triumph as each wicket went down. Other news was crowded off the front pages of the evening papers; people sat by their radio sets with their fingers crossed as each ball was bowled.

On the final morning, everything depended on Washbrook, the last 'recognized' batsman. Could he somehow produce a miracle – stay put, and play out time for a draw?

The answer to that hope was swift and devastating. Without adding to his score, he played too late to a yorker from Ramadhin. The rest of the innings collapsed. For the first time the West Indies had won a Test in England – and by the handsome margin of 326 runs. Between them, Ramadhin and Valentine had taken 18 wickets. And a song went into cricketing history – a song which West Indies supporters still revive in moments of triumph. Those two bowlers will never be forgotten, for each verse ends with the lines, 'Those two little pals of mine, Ramadhin and Valentine!'

BERT TRAUTMANN

Fifty thousand in the stands, three minutes left for play – and the match never finished. For the crowds burst over the barriers, surrounded one of the goal-keepers, and carried him shoulder-high off the field in a roar of cheering.

That goalkeeper was a man who had spent his first years in Britain behind barbed wire, and had been booed when he first appeared on a soccer field.

Bert Trautmann, captured German soldier, was not released from a prisoner of war camp until well after the end of World War Two. He joined Manchester City, outlived the boos of those who still resented all Germans, and played a big part in taking Manchester City to a Cup Final against Birmingham City at Wembley.

And then came disaster. Birmingham struggling to avoid defeat, attacked hard. An opponent crashed into Trautmann, both men went down, but Trautmann did not get up again. Manchester City's Cup triumph was marred by the news that their goalkeeper's neck was broken.

It looked like the end of Trautmann's soccer career. But within a few months he was walking about slowly and stiffly, grinning cheerfully when asked how he was getting on. In the late autumn the doctors finally said they were satisfied. The injury had healed. Trautmann looked at them anxiously. 'But will I be able to play again?'

'That's up to you,' they told him. 'Go and find out.'

So with T.V. cameras surrounding him, 162 days

after the accident, Bert Trautmann rejoined the team in training. He trotted slowly round the edge of the field. Then, suddenly, he sprinted towards the trainer. The trainer hesitated a moment, then hurled a ball at him – a hard throw at stomach height.

This was the moment.

A broken neck is a very serious injury. Would Trautmann falter, afraid that the jarring force of stopping the ball would reopen the injury? That was the question in every mind as the ball tore towards him.

Bert Trautmann gathered it up, grinned, and flung it back with all his old power and accuracy – winning back his place as City's goalkeeper for another eight years.

And so it was no wonder that his final match, a 'friendly' between a Combined Manchester team and an International XI, was never allowed to finish, and that the crowds he had entertained for so long swarmed on to the field to show their appreciation.

JAROSLAV DROBNY

CROSS country running in the springtime mud, a marathon in tropical heat, or 15 rounds for the world heavyweight championship are all tough on stamina and determination, but top-class tennis can run them pretty close. Certainly it did at a quarter to five on Thursday, 25th June, 1953, the occasion on which Budge Patty of the United States faced Jaroslav Drobny, the Czech player who had taken Egyptian nationality, across the net in the Wimbledon singles.

Both were experienced players; both knew what a test of endurance Wimbledon could be. Both had sampled the long, slow, heartbreaking struggle to the top. Both men were strong and accurate in service. Drobny took the first set 8–6. But the second set was the one which hinted to the crowd that drama was to come. Game followed game without either player being able to forge ahead. At the 29th, Patty saved at set point; Americans let out a cheer. They let out another when he did the same in the 31st. And finally he produced a perfect cross-court backhand volley which took Drobny – a left-hander – completely by surprise. Patty took the set with this stroke, at 18–16.

The long set had sapped Drobny's strength. He went down tamely, 6–3, in the third set, but he recovered in the fourth, winning it 8–6.

The two men looked at one another grimly. Hours had passed; the light was beginning to fade. There was every excuse for asking that the rest of the match be held over until the following day. But each man felt his own stamina would last longer than that of his opponent; they played on. Drobny took Patty's service in the first game. Lathered with sweat, they found they had used all the water in the urn beneath the umpire's ladder, and more had to be brought. Refreshed, Drobny went out and gained a lead of 3–1, only to find himself suddenly gripped by cramp. In agony, he tried jumping up and down at the base line to counteract it, but it slowed his reactions to Patty's service. Patty, spotting this, began placing his serves in a way that forced Drobny to cover a lot of ground – but just as he was beginning to fight back with points gained in this way he, too, felt a crippling pain in his right leg. In spite of this, he took Drobny's service in the eighth game. Drobny had to fight off a match point when he served at 5 6, and standing 15–40.

They struggled to 10–all. Which man would collapse first?

It was Patty. He lost his service in the 21st. Revived, he faced Drobny for the 22nd. At each serve, he struggled to wring a last response from mind and muscles which were too exhausted. A great roar went up as Drobny played a love game to take the match. It had lasted 4 hours and 20 minutes, one of the longest on record. For both players, and for the crowd of 15,000, it had been one to remember for ever.

MIKE HAILWOOD

A VETERAN motor-cyclist dashed forward from the crowd in the Isle of Man to congratulate the dust-stained man on the roaring Honda. Stanley Woods, winner of the Manx T.T. ten times between 1923 and 1939, was acknowledging his defeat by Mike Hailwood, who had just won his twelfth race over the winding, gruelling course that only an expert can master.

Most professional motor cyclists went into the sport because of the big prize money. But Mike Hailwood was the son of a near-millionaire. The jutting chin and the determined grin became famous in the nineteen-sixties on every track from Sachsenring in East Germany to Monza in Italy, but most of all in the Isle of Man, where he scored his greatest triumphs.

In 1964 he was taken ill with a throat infection four days before the Senior T.T. Doctors said it would be lunacy for him to get out of bed and take part in the race, but he defied them. Pale and drawn, he climbed on to an Italian M.V. Agusta, gave the crowd a tremendous performance which had them yelling his name as he came in to the chequered flag, and won at an average speed of 100.95 miles an hour. In a later race he pushed the record up to 105.62.

His greatest race came after he had already taken more than 60 'spills' in his career. There he was once more, lined up for the start of the Senior T.T., wearing the shabby old black leather riding suit which brought him luck. Ahead of him was the hardest course in the world, with deceptive high speed sections followed by sudden drops and hairpin bends needing split second accuracy in gear changes to avoid disaster. His target was not only the first prize. There was a personal duel involved, with his friend and rival Giacomo Agostini.

The start of such a race is a lonely moment for every rider. No matter how many times he has raced before, cold fear grips him in the stomach. And for Hailwood on this occasion there was extra reason for fear – the big six-cylinder Honda, he knew, would be difficult to handle on the bends. Agostini's M.V. Agusta would have the advantage.

It did. Mike found himself dropping back. Then one of those minor disasters caused by a mechanical fault held him up at the pits – his throttle grip had come loose, which meant that precious seconds were lost while the bolts were tightened.

He was now almost half a minute behind his rival!

Then came the greatest ride Hailwood ever achieved. Within two laps he made up all the lost ground, and was a second in front! Experts said nobody had ever ridden the T.T. course so brilliantly.

Perhaps the explanation is that Hailwood, not needing the prize money, had no fear of losing. And that gave him the freedom to concentrate on winning.

FAMILIAR as a cricket umpire in recent years is a man who in his youth set up one of cricket's most remarkable records.

It was 1938. Arthur Fagg was in his 8th professional season with Kent, and nothing was going right for him. With much more hope than expectation, while looking at the Colchester pitch before a match with Essex, he said to his captain, 'Wouldn't it be pleasant to run up a hundred before lunch, then double it by tea-time!'

It was just an idle wish.

It still seemed no more than that when he faced up to the Essex bowlers, worried, and a little lacking in confidence. But then to his surprise the runs started coming. They were rapid runs, mostly in fours; suddenly it was lunch, and he was 110 not out – a rare enough achievement in itself. Most batsmen believe they have done remarkably well to achieve a century before lunch, but this was nothing to what was to come. All afternoon Fagg batted on, and was 204 not out when tea came. Finally he was out for 244.

What had begun as a despairing attempt to end a run of bad luck had turned into the match of his career. In later years, people often asked what had got into him, but he could give no explanation. While Essex batted, he waited impatiently for his second knock. When Kent took their second innings he marched out to make 100 in less than an hour – a spectacular show of rapid scoring. The Colchester ground filled up as the news travelled, and people sneaked away from work and school to catch a glimpse of the drives, the chanceless strokes to leg, with which Arthur Fagg sent the ball streaking time and again to the boundary. Fagg had his eye in; no bowling changes unsettled him, and he raced on to make 202 not out – thus completing the only double century in each innings in the history of first class cricket. And this was straight after four matches which had yielded him a grand total of fewer than 20 runs!

In 'Wisden', the cricket annual, the record stands proudly alone after more than 30 years. And it is such an extraordinary one that it may well stand alone for another 30.

DON THOMPSON

He had all kinds of nicknames because he was so small. The Italians called him 'Il Topo', or 'The Mouse'. Don Thompson was only 5 feet 5½ inches tall. In the 50 kilometres walk at the Melbourne Olympics in 1956 he collapsed from the heat, and though he was a popular figure at the Rome Olympics in 1960, nobody expected him to do any better.

But Don Thompson had learned his lesson about heat. He had guessed it might be too hot for him in Rome, too. So, long in advance, he installed a home-made Turkish bath in his home near London. Week by week he built up the temperature, using kettles, an electric fire, and a gas boiler, until it reached 100° Fahrenheit. Then, in this heat, he 'worked out' in a track suit for 45 minutes.

In Rome, he lined up with 38 other starters, who included the reigning champion, Read of New Zealand, the 1952 champion, Dordoni of Italy, and the 1948 champion, Ljunggren of Sweden.

Two Indians raced off into a long lead, but Thompson was aware they could not hope to keep up the pace. After 12 kilometres they were faltering; for a short while Thompson found himself lying second, but then he was overtaken by two Australians and a Russian. One of the Indians was still in the lead. Suddenly, just as The Mouse was beginning to feel the strain of keeping on the heels of the others, the whole situation altered. The Russian and one of the Australians were disqualified and the other Australian, with the surviving Indian, pushed the pace too fast and almost collapsed with the effort.

The Mouse looked round him in astonishment! He was the leader by a huge margin. At the half-way stage his nearest rival was the 40-year-old Ljunggren, a full minute behind.

But at 35 kilometres he could hear the Swede's heavy breathing right at his shoulder, and there was nothing he could do to stop Ljunggren overtaking. The Swede sailed past with a cheerful grin, and British supporters resigned themselves to only a Silver Medal.

But then came the astonishing news that at 40 kilometres Thompson was in the lead again! At 45 kilometres he was 18 seconds in front. The excitement mounted. Ljunggren was famous as a fast finisher. Could he win back the lead in the last long battle to the line?

Thompson came pounding into the stadium to the cheers of the crowd. Twenty seconds later in came Ljunggren at a pace which seemed fast enough for him to overtake, even though there was only a single lap of the track to the line. But Thompson realized his danger. Somehow he summoned a last reserve, almost matching the speed of his rival. No longer did the gap narrow, and The Mouse reached the line 17 seconds in front, in a new Olympic record time.

The home-made Turkish bath had paid off!

JEAN BOROTRA

In the late nineteen-sixties a remarkable tennis player could still be seen in action in the Veterans' Championships at London's Queens Club. Jean Borotra, and his doubles partner 'Toto' Brugnon, were celebrating fifty years together in top tennis!

Borotra once explained how in his seventies he still retained the physique of a twenty year old. 'On the Western Front in the First World War you either kept fit or you died. It taught me to keep up physical training every morning.'

Borotra learned his tennis as a teenager on holiday in England. After returning from the trenches, he shot to the top, winning Wimbledon in 1924 and 1926, and with various partners took the doubles in 1925, 1932, and 1933.

The doubles successes were largely thanks to Borotra's technique which provided far greater 'cover' of the court than any players had achieved before. Constant play, as France's winning Davis Cup team, built up an understanding between Borotra and Brugnon which was so complete that opponents despaired of penetrating what seemed like a wall of men blocking every shot. Both were light on their feet, able to move across the court as swiftly as they could advance and retreat between the base line and the net. Their heyday was before the era of the smash serve. Each point had to be fought for – and the faster became the fight, the less likely these two were to lose.

When the smash serve changed the style of play, Borotra summed it up: 'The game's reached the point at which it has stopped before it has really begun. But you can't just put the clock back. You can't ask players to send down a slower service, and it would be no answer to use softer balls. To recreate the kind of tennis we've enjoyed playing, the best idea would be to take back the service line to about a yard behind the base line.'

It could happen.

DOROTHY HYMAN

THERE is an old, worn passport, with the name 'Dorothy Hyman' on the cover, which sums up the successes of the former captain of England's women's athletics team in a nutshell. Inside it are rubber stamp marks for a dozen countries in which in the nineteen fifties and early sixties she proved that lack of top class training facilities at home need not keep Britain from athletics triumphs.

Dorothy was the daughter of a Yorkshire coal miner, and when she was 13 she used to hurry home from school and then go out to train at her local track even in semi-darkness and freezing midwinter weather. Neighbours thought she was crazy, but her father did not. With his encouragement, she won the English Schools Junior 100 yards championship when she was 15. But training was a big problem. Not for her the easy life of the promising athletes in Russia and America. Only her coach and the two or three friends who ran with her as pacemakers knew what determination went into the making of Dorothy Hyman, Captain of Britain! By 1957, at the age of 16, Dorothy had won her place in international athletics, and in the following year at the Commonwealth Games she won a Gold Medal. The 1960 Olympics brought her Silver and Bronze Medals in Rome.

Two years later, at the European Games in Belgrade, she won the 100 metres Gold Medal, the 200 metres Silver Medal, and a Bronze for her part in the 4×100 metres relay. Later in the same year, at the Commonwealth Games at Perth, she won two Golds, for the 100 yards and the 220. Her homecomings were fiesta days in the mining village of Cudworth, and the National Coal Board, for whom she worked, presented her with a bracelet which included gold miniatures of all her medals.

In 1962 Dorothy was voted Athlete of the Year. The 1964 Olympics became her final target before retirement—but barely four months before the Games were due to begin, she pulled a thigh muscle. For all sportsmen and women, the greatest fear is the unlucky accident which will rob them of their winning chances, and for Dorothy Hyman this was a bitter disappointment. She had set her heart on one last attempt at the Olympic sprints.

Any doctor will agree that determination is worth more than massage. Dorothy gritted her teeth and *willed* her way back to fitness. Named as Britain's captain, she announced that Tokyo would be her final competition, a 'do or die' attempt to bring back one last medal for her collection.

And she did – with a Bronze for Britain's third place in the relay.

NAT LOFTHOUSE

Bolton Wanderers, the club for which Nat Lofthouse played from the age of 16 until his retirement at 35, was a very different club in the nineteen-fifties from the one it is now. With a record of seven Cup Final appearances and four Cup wins, Bolton had a tradition of packing nearly 70,000 people into their Burnden Park ground. They were a hard-playing club in the First Division, with queues at the turnstiles whenever they played at home.

Nat Lofthouse was the hero of every schoolboy for miles around. Capped 33 times for England, at one time he shared with Tom Finney of Preston the record for the number of goals scored for England – 29. For Bolton, he scored more than 250 goals in League matches alone. When Bolton won the F.A. Cup in 1958, he scored both the goals by which they beat Manchester United in the Final. The second of those two goals provoked plenty of argument, for Nat went into the United goalmouth not only with the ball, but with United's goalkeeper Gregg as well, such was the power of his attack!

It was the same driving force close to goal that won Nat his nickname, 'The Lion of Vienna', in 1952, and made him one of the most memorable figures in English soccer. The match against Austria was a tough one – not a dirty one, but the kind which is often described as 'robust', meaning that players took risks. Nat Lofthouse played a far-ranging game. He seemed to be in every tackle, showing inexhaustible stamina.

Suddenly he broke loose from a harrying trio of Austrians in midfield, resisted two hard frontal tackles as he raced down towards goal, and then accepted a headlong collision with the advancing goalkeeper as the price to pay for the shot he wanted – a quick flip into the corner of the net.

The goalmouth collision brought him down with an ugly gash in his leg – and brought him up shoulder high when cheering England fans rushed on to the field after the game.

Nat risked injury every time he charged a goalkeeper to buy a goal at the price of a collision, and finally the brutal treatment he gave himself took its toll. He retired through injury at a time when his speed and skill were still at their height.

FRED ARCHER

THE time – the eighteen-sixties. William Archer, re-tired steeplechase jockey and now landlord of the King's Arms in the Gloucestershire village of Prestbury, made up his mind to apprentice his son, Fred. There was not much doubt where Fred should go; for years, young Archer had been missing school three days a week to ride anything that stood on four legs. So, eleven years old, he was sent to Newmarket, to Matthew Dawson, then at the start of his triumph as a flat-race trainer. Dawson gave Archer the chance he needed; within a couple of years he had his first winner – taking a two year old, Athol Daisy, confidently into the lead in a nursery handicap.

A few people began to take notice of him. What sort of person was this rather long and narrow-faced youth? He was quiet, at one moment wildly generous, at the next, grimly thrifty. He was tall even then – 5 feet 8½ inches. There were those who warned he was too tall for a jockey. But in 1872, at least, he had no difficulty in making the weight of 5 stone 7 lbs. to win the Cesare-witch on a troublesome horse, Salvanos, who had re-cently overpowered a lightweight jockey. It was Fred's first big success; more followed so quickly that by 1874 he was champion jockey – an honour he held until his death – and retainers were coming in from all directions. But already, in the spring of 1874, there was a hint of the trouble ahead. By the autumn it took a starvation diet to get him down to 6 stone 1 lb. for the Cesarewitch and, at 3 lbs overweight, he was beaten by a head. The strain had left him too weak to win. But earlier in the year he had won the Lincoln and the 2,000 Guineas.

From 1875 onwards he was riding well over 200 winners a year. There were Derbies and Legers – but at terrible cost. For breakfast Archer now dared no more than gulp down a spoonful of hot castor oil and half an orange. His dinner was a sardine. More triumphant seasons; 220 winners, 210, 232, 241 and 246 – the last including his greatest Derby. Fred kept the colt Melton nearly last, knowing his greatest rival would be Paradox, a difficult horse to manage, and one which hated to make the running. On Melton, Archer moved up only slowly, leaving Paradox well in the lead. And presently he saw what he had hoped to see – Paradox becoming restless on his own. Archer brought Melton a little closer. Paradox became more restless, more conscious of being alone and out of sight of a single horse. And then – 150 yards from home – Archer made his challenge. Drawing up, he raced towards the post. With 50 yards to go, Paradox had the best of it; even three strides from the post he appeared to be a winner by a head. It was in the last bound that Melton sprang in front to win in what has been called the world's greatest feat of jockeyship.

It was Archer's last big victory. The next year Archer found the weight battle too much. With every ounce sweated off, he caught a chill, and ended his own life. Nat Gould, perhaps the greatest of all racing writers, described him as 'a man done to death by his own profession'.

GEORGE BEST

Every generation of schoolboys has its soccer hero, and George Best has held this position longer than most. Without any doubt one of the most brilliant ball players of all time, Best was born in Belfast in 1947, and his career has already gained him a house which cost £35,000. Not all of this has come directly from football; his annual income of about £20,000 also comes from two shops he has bought, and from advertising.

But what is now a financial empire began with nothing more than a few shillings in the pocket of a boy starting out as a soccer professional. In 1965 George Best was a shy, rather hesitant boy. It took two League Championships and a European Cup win with Manchester United to make him into a public figure, with his name as much a household word as was that of Stanley Matthews twenty years earlier.

Irish temperament makes him oscillate between brilliant football and intolerably bad behaviour on the field – behaviour which has forced referees to book him eight times, and send him off. But even at his worst moments he has seldom lost the sympathy of the crowd – and even when he has, it has been won back swiftly by his entertaining play. In 1968 he was voted both English and European Player of the Year, and in the European Cup Final of that year he demonstrated the reason why. Wriggling with great speed through the strong Benfica defence, he was confronted by the Portuguese goal-keeper Henriques, off his line in order to narrow the angle of Best's shot. Most players would have taken a chance, and relied on a shot combining power and accuracy within the narrow angle left open.

But not Best.

With complete calm, ignoring the full-throated yell from the crowd of 100,000, he took the ball *round* Henriques, so swiftly that he caught the goalkeeper on the wrong foot. From his new position, with a wide open goal, he had only to tap the ball into the net!

ANN PACKER

Ann Packer went to the Tokyo Olympics in 1964 as British record holder for 440 yards, and with her fiancé Robbie Brightwell in the same team. She started well, winning her 400 metres heat in the second fastest time so far that year, and beating her chief rival, Betty Cuthbert of Australia, into second place. But in the final she had the bad luck to be drawn in lane 6, which meant running blind, with all the others concealed behind her, She had to be content with a Silver Medal. Hiding her disappointment, she pinned her hopes on Robbie Bright-well providing them with a Gold Medal to hang up in their future home. But he could come only fourth in the men's 400 metres.

Had their chance gone? It certainly seemed so. The 400 had been the event in which both had specialized.

But Ann had another individual race to come. It was the 800 metres. This was a distance she had only run six times before in competition! She had no real idea of the best tactical approach, knowing very little about pace-setting or how to avoid getting boxed in. She had qualified to compete in the Olympic 800 only at the very last moment, and had not given much thought to it until she saw Robbie beaten in his race. It was then, she said afterwards, that she determined to try to win it.

She tensed herself for the start of what was to be her last Olympic race – facing a last chance that by all athletics standards was no chance at all. The final comment about her career had already been written in the world's press.

After 120 metres she was lying 6th, but seemed to be running quite strongly. At the bell, she was still at the back, which surprised nobody. Maryvonne Dupureur, the French champion, was the favourite to win, and as they came away from the back straight she was leading.

It was then that Ann knew she had the stamina to win. But how could she break away? Another runner was just to the outside of her, and there seemed no way through.

Suddenly Ann slackened pace, swung out in an arc, and shot round the final bend on the outside. It seemed an almost suicidal thing to do, but she had done it. And it was paying off! From 6th to 4th – all the time she was accelerating, sprinting like the wind into a final 100 metres which was one of the greatest memories of Tokyo. Maryvonne Dupureur struggled to hold her lead – and could not. She looked weary as Ann swept past her in a Gold-winning burst towards the tape. The stadium roar swelled to a crescendo, as breasting the tape, Ann ran on into the arms of her fiancé, with a world record behind her, and the warmest feelings for her future from everyone there with a shred of romance in their nature!

TERRY DOWNES

IT took Terry Downes just twenty professional fights in a year and a half to make him British Middleweight Champion. A Londoner who had served in the American Marines, he had returned to Britain as a top amateur, and the moment he turned professional he set his sights on the World Championship, held by Paul Pender of the United States.

He got his chance to meet Pender in January 1961. Downes fought him in Boston – and took a beating which must have shocked him after his steady journey to the top.

But a few months later, in England, Downes won the return fight, forcing Pender to retire after nine rounds. This time he made no mistakes, and never let the American penetrate his defence. His hand was held high as the fight ended, and the huge crowd at Wembley cheered him as the new World Champion.

It was now that Downes's troubles began. For an American, the rewards of being at the top in boxing are high. There is no shortage of opponents, and every fight brings in enough money to pay the heavy bills for managers, sparring partners, gymnasium hire, and travel. For an Englishman, the bills are just as high – but the rewards are not.

Pender regained the World title in April 1962, and later that year Downes was stripped of his British title for failing to defend it. In search of fights at a fair price, Downes moved up into the light-heavyweights. But even there the bills often came in faster than the money. The climax came in November 1964. Once again Terry Downes had battled his way to the top, and in Manchester he entered the ring to fight America's Willie Pastrano for the World Light-heavyweight title. He was beaten in the eleventh round, but those who said it was simply a case of Pastrano being the better man were wrong. On the money side, the American was paid something in the region of £30,000 for defending the title – enough to settle all his training bills and leave a handsome profit. Terry Downes's share was £3,000.

No wonder that two months later when he discovered that for a return fight the price would still be the same, Downes threw in the towel. There has to be fair play outside the ring, as well as inside it.

ERIC LIDDELL

Edinburgh's Eric Liddell goes down in sporting history as the man who proved the experts wrong. When officials and other runners saw him, they roared with laughter as he flailed his way along with his head flung back and his arms racing to and fro as if he were training with a punchball in readiness for a big boxing match. What brought him success was his amazing strength. He won his races in spite of his style.

Liddell also broke all the rules of running by the manner in which he decided to specialize in the quarter mile. He began as a sprinter, winning a number of championships and finally setting up a British 100 yards record in 1924. In his first 440 yards race he collided with another runner just after the start and was knocked flying. Instead of being resigned to losing the race, he leaped to his feet, far behind the field, and tore after them so fast that he went sailing through to find himself the winner!

For the 1924 Olympics, he was regarded as Britain's Number One for the 100 metres. But Eric, who had strong religious views, backed out when he heard the heats were to be run on Sunday. He decided to enter for the 400 metres instead. American coaches who watched him during the heats for the 400 metres were convinced that because of his unorthodox style he would be no danger to their runners. 'You *can't* run 400 metres that way!' they said. 'Nobody's ever done it.'

There has to be a first in everything.

When the final came, Liddell, in the sixth lane, set off at a stupendous pace, and was four yards ahead of his nearest rivals at the half-way mark. This, said the experts hurriedly, was ridiculous. The man could not possibly hope to win.

They were proved wrong about 25 seconds later. In spite of a tremendous spurt by one of the Americans, Liddell held on. He came through the tape with a lead of three yards, to set up a new Olympic record.

'How did you do it?' the officials asked in astonishment. 'Where did you get the reserve for your final spurt?'

'Goodness knows,' panted Liddell modestly. 'I suppose I must have started my spurt when the pistol went!'

FRANK TYSON

THERE is no other competition in the world which makes England writhe and groan quite so much as a Test series against Australia. And the 1954 series could hardly have begun in a worse manner, for in the First Test England had been soundly thrashed. Could anybody produce a Christmas present for England in the Second Test, at the famous Sydney Oval?

The Australians did not think so. England, sent in to bat, were barracked by jeering voices from up on the Hill, the slope at Sydney which attracts the roughest, toughest, least respectful crowd in the world. England's top batsmen were Len Hutton, Peter May, Trevor Bailey, Bill Edrich and Colin Cowdrey. A notable list of names, yet out they all went, skittled swiftly for a total of 154. In England, thousands of people got up early, sat in their dressing gowns in rooms already decorated for Christmas, and listened to the fading and crackling short-wave broadcast of the match. A Christmas present of an England victory seemed a thin hope.

But then, on the second day, Australia failed to hammer home their advantage and were out for 228. When England batted again, May and Cowdrey renewed the hopes of those listening back home. The total was 296, which left Australia needing 223 to win. England's hope for a draw depended on keeping down Australia's scoring rate, so that the runs could not be made in the time that was left.

Nobody had reckoned with Tyson; 25 year old Frank Tyson, the Lancashireman who played for North-

amptonshire and who had just got up from a hospital
bed after a head injury. Most England fans thought he
should have stayed there, that he had not recovered
enough to play.

But now, in partnership with Brian Statham, Tyson
made his name as a Test bowler. Each took a wicket by
close of play, to make Australia 72 for 2.

And then, next morning, with his second over of the
day, Tyson began to deliver his Christmas present to the
listening supporters back in England. A yorker sent back
the tough, defensive batsman Burke, another got the
stylish Graeme Hole out third ball. 77 for 4! Then
Tyson, as a square leg catcher, held a 'skier' while running, and out went Ritchie Benaud, 102 for 5! After
lunch, out went Archer. 122 for 6! Statham helped by
sending back Davidson. 127 for 7. In his place came
Lindwall, the man who had bowled the bumper which
injured Tyson. Revenge was swift: 136 for 8. Statham
got Langley and it was 145 for 9.

Neil Harvey hit out, but at 184 Tyson made Bill
Johnston slide a catch to the ever-ready Godfrey Evans
behind the wicket.

Tyson, with 6 for 85, had given England a Christmas
present of a handsome victory!

DOROTHY TYLER

MARY RAND, Lillian Board, Dorothy Hyman and Dorothy Tyler are without doubt Britain's top women athletes of the century. Dorothy never won a 'Gold' – but she deserved one for determination. As a 15 year old schoolgirl, she burst into the news with high jumps of 5 feet, and in 1936 she surprised the Olympic selectors with a British record of 5 feet 4. At the Berlin Olympics the slim schoolgirl stood out among her opponents – who decreased in numbers rapidly once the bar was raised above 5 feet. At 5 feet 3 she was one of a final quintet. Dorothy sailed over at her first attempt, but the others faltered badly. A French girl dropped out, and so did a German.

The bar went up by $\frac{3}{4}$ of an inch. All three failed, so, in accordance with Olympic rules, on they went, jump after jump, until somebody finally got over. It was a Hungarian, and Dorothy had to be content with the Silver Medal for second place.

Perhaps 'content' is not the right word, for though in the years that followed she married and had two children, Dorothy still had her eyes on the Olympics. She pushed the British record up above 5 feet 5 – and waited.

She had a very long wait – twelve years, because of World War Two. But in spite of this long break, she was in such good form that she was picked for the Wembley Olympics in 1948.

At 5 feet $4\frac{1}{2}$, she was again one of three survivors. All three cleared the bar. At 5 feet $5\frac{1}{4}$, one rival dropped out. The bar went to 5 feet $6\frac{1}{8}$.

This was now a grim struggle between Britain and America. Both jumpers could be considered veterans, for the American, Alice Coachmann, had also been jumping since before the war.

The American cleared the bar at the new height. There was a tense silence throughout the huge crowd as Dorothy made her run-up. She rose high into the air in what seemed to be the start of a perfect jump – but she failed!

Without hesitation she went back to her mark, tried again, and was over.

But that first failure cost her the Gold Medal. Both women were too tired to jump any higher, so the American won, having cleared the bar at the first attempt. Once again, after 12 years, Dorothy was second. But she had one consolation. She shared the Olympic record.

For most people this would have been enough. But Dorothy Tyler was not satisfied until she had turned out *twice again* to become the only woman who has ever represented British athletics in four Olympic Games!

JACQUES ANQUETIL

Cold calculation is sometimes the recipe for reaching the top in sport. When Jacques Anquetil won the Tour de France for the fifth time, the crowds did not know whether to cheer or to groan. The popular kind of Tour winner is the man who gains his lead on the tough stretches through the mountains. The crowds worship the rugged rider who sweats his way up the steep slopes struggling past one rival after another, then sails triumphantly down the other side.

Anquetil never won that way. What gained him an income of about £35,000 a year was his mastery of the time trials. In a race like the Tour de France, run in 22 daily stages over a 2,000 mile route, time trials are vitally important. In the mountains, Anquetil did not tire himself out trying to beat the leaders; instead, he took it easy, a bit behind – but not more behind than he knew he could pick up again in the time trial.

But his fifth win, in 1964, nearly proved his undoing.

Even his cold calculation almost went wrong against the tough opposition of Raymond Poulidor, a fellow Frenchman. At the start of the final day's stage, Anquetil found he was leading Poulidor by only 14 seconds which, in his view, was far too little for safety. He wanted to save his strength for the final time trial, but it was obvious he would have to go flat out in the $73\frac{1}{2}$ mile road race from Odense to Versailles, which came first – otherwise the muscular and speedy Poulidor would snatch the lead.

But uneasily he became aware that the gap was narrowing! Behind him, Poulidor was riding a 'blinder', one of those rare moments when speed comes without effort, and the bike seems to be a part of the body. Anquetil, angry with himself for his over-confidence, gradually won back his lead, but at the cost of exhaustion.

And now came the 17 mile time trial. Nobody in the world could beat Anquetil in a time trial. The only Frenchman that day who was not so sure was Anquetil himself! Only he knew what that earlier struggle had cost him in reserves of speed and stamina.

The time trial is a race against the stopwatch instead of against other riders. Riders go off at intervals of two minutes. Without rivals in sight to whip up the speed, many competitors have no idea whether they are doing well or not. This was where Anquetil's cool calculation had won him event after event. Through the Paris streets he rode, watched by thousands of his expert fellow-countrymen, many of them armed with stop-watches and as closely aware of what he had to do as Anquetil himself.

And as he rode up to the finish, Anquetil calculated he had kept up a speed of exactly 27 miles an hour.

His confidence was justified. He had actually *gained* time, in spite of his exhausting battle in the morning, and had won his fifth Tour not by 14 seconds, but by 55!

JACK HOBBS

A YEAR or two ago, in a end of the cricket season Festival match at Scarborough, an up and coming England opener came off at the tea interval grinning, perhaps a shade smugly, because he had knocked up a big score.

An old cricket supporter took the grin off his face. 'Aye, tha' can smile,' he said, 'but Jack would've got them runs in *half* the time.'

He was probably right.

Jack Hobbs, born in 1882, was a fast scorer in school games when he was 12. When he grew up he offered his services to Essex – who still groan at the memory of how they turned him down – and then went to Surrey in 1905, staying with them for 29 years, during which time he set up two records that take some beating; 61,237 runs and 197 centuries.

Hobbs was at his greatest when partnered for England by Herbert Sutcliffe, of Yorkshire, 12 years his junior. The partnersip began in 1924, when the two men opened against South Africa, and it lasted through 38 Tests. It depended on a mastery of every stroke in the batting repertoire. Over the years, it became almost impossible to send down a ball which either of them would find unplayable. They played on bowlers' weaknesses, by adapting the old technique normally used for sheltering a 'tail-ender' from the bowling. If Hobbs found he could demoralize a certain bowler by repeatedly hitting his leg-side deliveries for four, then Sutcliffe would ensure a single or a three when necessary to put Hobbs back in the crease at the right moment.

They revelled in difficult wickets. A Brisbane 'sticky-dog' – when the sun beats down on turf soaked by a semi-tropical storm – has destroyed countless England batsmen because the ball comes up unpredictably from the pitch. But Hobbs and Sutcliffe, with their tremendous range of strokes, could adapt themselves to this. Arriving at the wicket to open for England, they would prod the surface with their bats, perhaps even reach down and press the surface with their finger tips. They would exchange glances, give a brisk nod to the bowlers – and then England were away to a flying start.

No fewer than 15 times when they opened for England they put a century on the board before their stand was broken!

HARRY CARR

THE world's top jockeys are a very short and select list, and Harry Carr well deserves his place on it. Jockey to royalty for 18 years, he proved time and again his skill, courage, and above all his patience, which is the most important factor in handling a highly-strung colt in classic races.

The careful breeding that makes a classic winner also makes a neurotic. Alcide, Harry Carr's mount in the 1958 St. Leger, was as temperamental as an opera star. Earlier in the season when Harry was going through all the painstaking work to prepare Alcide for the Derby, the colt threw him several times by suddenly rearing up on his hind legs. He was hot favourite for the Derby, but only a few days beforehand in a bout of extra wild enthusiasm he leaped so violently that he wrenched a stomach muscle and had to be withdrawn from the race.

After Alcide recovered, the new target became the St. Leger, and Harry Carr's big concern was learning to control the colt's sudden fits of temperament. Alcide ran brilliantly to win the Great Voltigeur Stakes at York, a few weeks before the St. Leger, and when the great day came, the big question was whether Carr could keep him equally well under control in this much more important race.

Carr had ridden many difficult horses in his time. Nobody becomes jockey to the Queen Mother, riding horses from the Boyd-Rochfort stable, without a lot of experience of everything that runs on four legs. In the parade before the start Alcide remained cool under

Carr's gently restraining hand, and took no notice of the noise of the crowd which so often unsettles a top flat racer.

When the race began, Alcide proved to be in a lazy mood. He settled down at the rear of the field, paying no attention to Harry Carr's attempts to wake him up. For half a mile he ran as if out for a gentle canter. And it was in this period that Harry Carr showed what a great jockey he was. Most would have used drastic methods to get the colt on the move, but after his first gentle attempt at persuasion, Carr let him carry on at his own speed.

And Alcide picked his own moment! Suddenly he took a firm hold of his bit, and leaped forward into the tremendous stride which made him the favourite among the racing crowds that summer. He swept into the lead without Carr touching him, and was 8 lengths in front at the winning post.

In riding, perhaps the true sign of greatness is knowing when to do nothing!

JIM REDMAN

A T.T. MOTORCYCLE race, for the winner, is a careful balance between speed and danger.

For Jim Redman, in 1963, extra factors were involved.

It was a searing hot day in the Isle of Man. The tar on the roads had melted, making the surface so deadly that more than twenty riders had parted company with their bikes. One rider's engine had run so hot it seized up, pitching him off at 120 miles an hour!

But Jim Redman was in the lead for the first time in a T.T., and determined to win! And when the third factor made its presence felt, a decision had to be made immediately.

It was an agonizing factor he had never encountered before. With each lap the engine of his 250 c.c. Honda grew hotter and hotter, until the searing heat was penetrating right through his leathers and burning his legs. Naturally, overheated, the engine was losing revs.

The choice was to race on, in agony and in danger of becoming the second rider to be pitched off by a seized engine, or pulling up at the pits at the half-way stage after three laps in the hope that the mechanics could find a cure.

When he stopped at the pits for petrol the mechanics begged him to let them try – but Redman, knowing how close behind him were his rivals, gulped a mouthful of lemon squash and shook his head.

The factors now involved were pain, speed, time, distance, the slippery road, and whether the engine would seize. Like a juggler, Redman had to keep them all in the air as he rode.

Lap by lap, the engine lost more revs and made more ominous noises. And behind him a rival was gaining steadily. On the slippery surface, Redman now had to take corners faster than he would normally dare, to make up for seconds lost through slow speed on the straight runs where a properly running engine would respond to the throttle.

On the last lap his teeth were clenched with the burning agony of his legs. On his final turn, the Honda almost slid away from him on a lake of molten tar, but somehow he managed to control it, and reached the chequered flag to win.

Slowing, he spread out his legs, away from the fiery heat.

Like the man who kept banging his head against the wall, 'it was so nice when he stopped'!

SYDNEY WOODERSON

'WE can't let him carry the Olympic flame,' the officials said. 'He doesn't *look* like an Olympic athlete.'

There was a row – but they were right. Sydney Wooderson, holder of world records, winner over distances ranging from 440 yards to 10 miles cross country, looked totally unlike a Greek God, and the men planning the 1948 Wembley Olympics finally picked a relatively unknown runner who did look the part.

But Sydney was a man who had been called Britain's most popular athlete. Small, with big horn-rimmed spectacles, he had at first been treated as a joke in international running. A cracked bone put paid to his chances in the 1936 Berlin Olympics, but the following year he set a new world record for the mile, followed in 1938 by world records for the half mile and 800 metres.

His greatest race without any doubt was the 5,000 metres in Oslo in 1946. Two days beforehand he again injured an ankle, but he showed no signs of it when he lined up alongside the 10,000 metres world record holder, Heino of Finland, at the start. The great Dutch runner Slykhuis was also in the field. Heino made the running, setting a tremendous pace, and at the end of the first lap Wooderson was lying twelfth – but exactly on the time schedule he had set himself. Only once in the first eleven laps was he down on his set times, and then by a mere second. Only once, again by one second, was he up. He ran an almost uncannily judged race. Unworried by the pace of the leaders, he progressively caught his field, until at the bell he came clear away from the opposition to win in 14 minutes 8.6 seconds.

No wonder in 1948 many people sharply criticized the Olympic planners, and protested that Wooderson had been robbed of his rightful place.

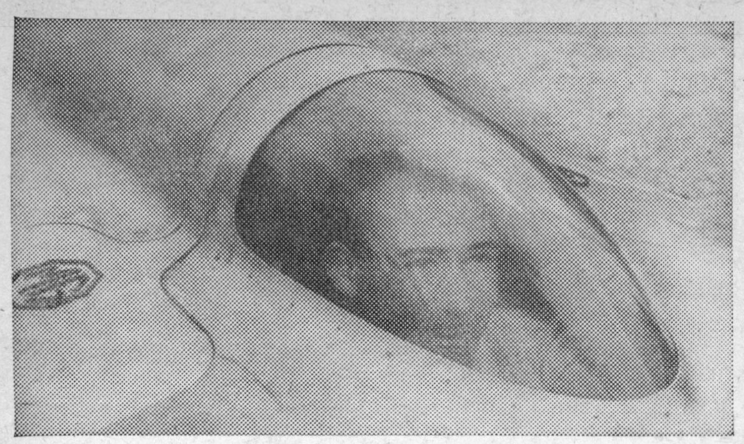

STIRLING MOSS

THE pale green Lotus Climax Formula 1 racing car shot off the track into the ditch, jacknifed, and trapped its driver by the legs for half an hour while doctors and firemen battled to free him.

That was in April 1962 at Goodwood. Eleven months later Stirling Moss announced his retirement from motor racing. After his recovery he had tried himself out, and discovered that his reactions were no longer swift enough for the perils of motor racing.

It was not his first crash. Stirling Moss had broken both legs and injured his back in a crash at 145 miles an hour in 1960, and the following year his car had spun off the track after a tyre burst. In all his years at the top, surprisingly the highest honour had eluded him. He had never been world champion, though for twelve years he had been the most consistently successful British driver. What prevented him was the long run of success by the Argentinian, Fangio.

Probably his greatest race was when he became the first home driver to win the British Grand Prix. He was second to Fangio in the team of four Mercedes cars competing against Coopers, Vanwalls, Ferraris, and Maseratis. Moss was in the front row at the start, with Fangio and a Maserati driven by Behra. Ninety laps ahead, each of 3 miles – and for nine laps the two Mercedes battled it out for first place, with Behra only a few yards behind – until suddenly he was out of it, with oil streaming from a broken pipe.

Out went a Cooper, two Vanwalls, three Connaughts, and a Ferrari, all with engine trouble caused by the killing pace set by the front runners. A Maserati driven by Musso replaced Behra's in third place, but not for long; another Mercedes took over. The fourth Mercedes moved into fourth place.

And as they came into the finish Moss, as Mercedes' Number Two driver, waved his leader past. But Fangio refused the signal to take the lead – recognizing that Moss, leader almost all the way, deserved the victory!

A lonely man by nature, in a lonely sport, Moss was a man who pleased the crowds, and brought about a British motor-racing revival. There were many who wished his retirement could have been postponed a few more years.

DIANE ROWE

On the eve of their 21st birthday, Diane Rowe and her twin sister Rosalind lay awake in a London hotel – victims of nerves! For the following day at Wembley they were to play in the final of the women's doubles in the table tennis World Championships. Diane tossed and turned, worried about being too exhausted in the morning to give the kind of performance needed.

In the morning came birthday wishes over the phone from home, but in spite of this they had a poor start to the day in their Mixed Doubles matches.

It was then that understanding friends took a hand. Diane and her sister were free during the afternoon, so their friends, seeing how tense they were, wisely concentrated on turning the day into a 21st birthday instead of a finals day. They talked about birthday presents, not the game. The result was that away from Wembley, Diane and Rosalind managed to become just a pair of twins who had that day become entitled to their own front door keys. Because of this, they had no time to work themselves up into a state of nervous tension, and they were relaxed and smiling when they came out in the evening for their final against Kathleen Best and Ann Haydon – the future Ann Jones of Wimbledon's Centre Court.

The twins lost their first game. Rosalind's nerves caught up with her again, and Diane, trying to cover up for her sister's lack of concentration, attempted shots which were impossible. But in the second game they romped home easily, and this gave them the relaxation they needed. They were trailing again in the third when suddenly Rosalind had a burst of brilliance, winning 5 points in a row when trailing 19–16.

The fourth game, therefore, was vital; every point was a battle, with Best and Haydon fighting gallantly to deny the twins victory.

Came the final point which would make Diane and her sister World Doubles Champions. Haydon smashed the ball across, forcing Diane to spin almost in a circle to counter it. As the crowd rose in their seats, she managed to play it – a vicious return that shot like a bullet though the narrow gap between Best's forearm and the table!

The Rowe twins had won their final point and the Championship – a terrific 21st birthday!

ARTHUR NEWTON

Right back at the start of the century, when athletes were for the first time beginning to ask what *was* the limit of human endurance, a young South African set himself the grisly task of running all day and all night to set a world record for 24 hours. Many people said it was impossible, which simply made Arthur Newton more determined to find out whether they were right.

They were wrong. Carefully conserving his energy, Arthur kept going at a steady pace, and was still firmly on his feet when the ordeal was over.

Nearly half a century later, Arthur Newton, at the end of a long career of competitive running and coaching, was still turning out long before dawn every morning to pound along the pavements of Ruislip in West London. He had a new target now, in his seventies – to complete 100,000 miles of running before he retired. Once again, he had picked a target most people thought impossible – a distance not so far short of half-way to the moon.

And once again, Arthur Newton achieved it! He was now in his seventies – and off he went for a final coaching and officiating tour in South Africa.

But throughout this time his world 24 hour record still stood. It was another South African, Wally Hayward, who decided to challenge it. He came to London to make the attempt, and at times during the day and night there were quite large crowds round the track to watch him, and cheer his success.

But they were also watching somebody else – a lean,

seventy year old runner who whenever Hayward started
to flag, joined in for a couple of laps to keep him in
conversation, hand him refreshments, and make sure
exhaustion did not sap his morale.

Guess who?

Jack Dempsey (left)

JACK DEMPSEY

WHEN Gene Tunney beat Jack Dempsey and became
World Heavyweight Champion, nearly a year went by
before he had a chance to defend the title. And the man
he found facing him in the ring once again was Jack
Dempsey!

Dempsey was 32, considerably older than Tunney. He
was also trying to do what no man had ever done –
regain the World Heavyweight title. It was a fighter
against a boxer; Dempsey had long been known as the
Manassa Mauler. Because of his habit of standing very
close to his opponent after a knockdown, ready to deliver
a final punch the moment the man was on his feet, a rule
was made for the fight, that if either boxer knocked his
opponent down he should retire to a neutral corner
during the referee's count.

Tunney was a cool, scientific boxer. He stayed cool for
four rounds, picking up points with occasional jabs

while Dempsey tried to force the pace with some wild hitting. After the fourth, Dempsey looked weak on his feet from over-exertion, but his seconds performed miracles, and he came out for the fifth both fresh and ferocious. Tunney was forced into retreat by a positive tornado of accurate punches. Dempsey kept it up in the sixth and seventh rounds, wearing Tunney down, forcing him to the ropes, and hunting for the chance to put in a knockout punch.

And at last he succeeded. It caught Tunney on the body, dazing him so that he had no defence against a flurry of punches to the cheeks and chin.

The ropes broke his fall, but down he went.

And Dempsey forgot the special rule! He stood a little to one side, and the warnings from his seconds were drowned by the noise from the crowd of 150,000.

It took the referee about four seconds – some say eight – to make Dempsey understand and move to a neutral corner. Only *then* did he start to count Tunney out.

And at 'nine', Tunney staggered to his feet, defended for the rest of the round, then coolly scored point after point in the remaining rounds. There was no doubt of his victory on points, but to this day most of the huge crowd who watched the fight more than forty years ago are convinced that Tunney was on the canvas for fourteen seconds or even more – and that the Manassa Mauler should have had the honour of being the first double winner of the World Heavyweight title.

DON BRADMAN

WHENEVER a young Australian batsman shows promise, the experts 'down under' look at him appraisingly and hopefully, in case they have another Bradman. And the man himself, Sir Donald Bradman, is still among the Test selectors to add his own very expert assessment.

The Bradman legend began in the late nineteen-twenties, which were great years for new Test stars. England produced Hammond and Leyland; Bradman was Australia's answer. In the Test series of 1928–9, he was Australia's top scorer with 468 runs in 8 innings. In 1930, when the Australians came to England, Bradman brought colour into the game with innings of 334, 254, 232, and 131. His 334 in the Third Test, at Leeds, was a record highest score by an Australian against England.

Though the quarrel about bodyline bowling marred the next series, in Australia, Bradman proved to

be the batsman best able to stand up to fast bowling of
this kind. Scores were lower in the bodyline matches, but
he was once again producing double and treble centuries
when the Australians came back to England in 1934,
and he took part in an amazing record stand of 451 for
the second wicket. This series put the Ashes firmly in
Australia's keeping, and the 1936–7 Tests kept them
there until long after the war, thanks again in great part
to double centuries from Bradman. The long gap had no
effect on him; he produced double centuries again in the
1946–7 series, and then, when nearly forty, he was third
in the batting averages in his final Test series, in 1948.

With a batting career like that, it is no wonder that
the Australians have never stopped searching for his successor.

JOHN PETRIE

IT is a certain kind of greatness to keep your name in
the record books for well over three-quarters of a century. This was the achievement of a quite humble outside-right, John Petrie of the Scottish team Arbroath.

Arbroath is a fishing port north east of Dundee with a
long though never brilliant record in the Scottish
League. In the 1885 Scottish Cup they found they were
drawn at home against Bon Accord, of Aberdeen, of
whom they had never heard. The day of the match was
appalling, rain had been falling for 48 hours, and the
pitch was a sea of mud. Bon Accord were half an hour
late – they had had only eight train tickets for eleven
players; the others had leaped from the moving train
outside the station and sneaked through the coal yards!
And when they came on to the field, there were scornful
shouts from the 600 Arbroath supporters. Instead of
soccer shirts and shorts, Bon Accord played in their
workers shirts and trousers held up with braces. They
played in ordinary walking shoes, too.

Somewhere, somebody had made a mistake! Somebody had failed to check up on Bon Accord, to find out
whether they had the equipment or the resources to play
in the Scottish Cup!

At the kick-off, Bon Accord's forwards rushed away –
and slipped! Without studded boots, they had no grip on
the greasy mud. As soon as they regained their feet, they
slipped again.

Outside-right John Petrie of Arbroath discovered
that all he had to do was change course as he dribbled

"

down the field – and all the defenders fell flat on their faces as they tried to do the same. By-passing the heap of muddy men of Bon Accord, he tapped the ball casually into the net as the goalkeeper slid along the ground on his waistcoat buttons.

Dejected, with wet feet and mud-caked trousers, Bon Accord slipped when they tried to kick, slipped when they tried to tackle, slipped when they tried to run, and even slipped when they tried to stand still. Goals came so fast that the referee had to borrow a notebook from a spectator in order not to lose count of the score, and admitted afterwards that there were 7 goals he disallowed 'out of pity'. Arbroath won the match 36–0, and 13 of the goals came from John Petrie.

And that 13 still stands as an all-time record in senior football!

Tom Molyneux was a Virginia slave early in the last century. He used his fists so well that an overseer called the plantation owner along to see him beat a bully unconscious. So impressed was the plantation owner that he vowed to match Tom in a prize fight. The prize, if he won, would be his freedom.

Tom fought, and won, and *did* gain his freedom. Not long afterwards, as champion of America, he crossed the world and was matched against Tom Cribb, the champion of England.

It was a mixed crowd that turned out at Copthall Common in Surrey to see that fight. Around the ringside were the men of title and fashion whose money made the prize ring the poor man's only hope of quick reward; behind them were 'The Caulies' – Britain's cauliflower-eared fighters there to watch and learn from their champion. They had only one thing in common – they were all for Tom Cribb, and for a British victory by fair means or foul! And they thought they had little to fear, as the referee was for Cribb, too. That had been 'attended to' in advance by gamblers with long purses and no scruples.

But as the fight developed, in the freezing cold of a winter's day, Tom Molyneux looked so much the better man that it seemed the referee would have to give an honest verdict. Beyond the ropes, men with big bets on Cribb eyed each other uneasily.

Cribb was weakening. The powerful ex-slave's iron-hard fists caught him time and again with his defences down. Suddenly Cribb staggered backwards, slipped to his knees, and fell. There was a shout of dismay as he struggled to rise, then sank back, exhausted and half-unconscious. Reluctantly, the referee started across to Tom Molyneux to award him victory.

In desperation, one ringside gambler whispered in the ear of his companion, who nodded quickly, then gave a loud bellow of anger. Blows were struck; one man fell into the ring. It was a put-up job to cause delay – and that delay, made before Molyneux had been given the verdict, gave Cribb the chance to recover. It also left the man from hot Virginia shivering in damp, icy English weather to which he had never been accustomed.

'Get to your feet!' yelled the crowd at Cribb. In the confusion, the man who had been 'knocked' into the ring put his arm under Cribb's shoulders. One report says he even poured brandy down the champion's throat. Cribb struggled to his feet, caught the shivering Molyneux with a hard rain of punches, and eventually beat him. It was a fight that did Britain no credit, and Molyneux swore revenge.

It took a long time coming. But more than a century later, in front of a fair-minded crowd and an honest referee, John Henry Lewis, the World Light-heavyweight title holder, came to England and beat Len Harvey, the British champion.

Lewis was Molyneux's great-great-nephew.

E. MCDONALD BAILEY

Unlike long-distance runners, sprinters seldom have more than one or two seasons at the top. But E. McDonald Bailey of Trinidad did well in the Amateur Athletics Association Championships in London in 1939, and returned in 1946, at the end of World War Two, as if there had been no gap of seven years in his running career.

During his career he achieved almost every success that a sprinter can hope for. Bailey won both the 100 and 220 yards in the 1946 A.A.A. Championships, and in the same season, running for Britain in an international against France, he equalled the British 100 yards record of 9.7 seconds, which had stood unchallenged for more than twenty years.

A new target for 'Mac' appeared in the following year when a visiting American set up a British All-Comers record of 9.6. Bailey promptly equalled it – and in the same season again scored the sprint double at the A.A.A. Championships.

The 1948 season was an unlucky one for him, but in spite of injuries and a throat infection he still managed to finish third in the A.A.A. 100 yards, as well as reaching the final of the Olympic 100 metres. He recovered completely by the following season, and in the next few years he not only returned to the habit of winning the A.A.A. sprint double, but won over 100 yards at almost every first class track in the country.

His recipe for winning was that of conserving himself for a tremendous burst in the final 20 yards. One of the

finest examples of this was in his sprint against France in
1946. Bailey was left at the start, and was more than a
yard behind after a third of the race. The positions remained the same for several seconds, and then suddenly
Bailey's body tensed and he appeared almost to *double*
his speed in an astonishing spurt that brought him right
past the rest of the field, to romp home with several feet
to spare.

Bobby Moore evades tackles by Willi Wallace (left) and Billy Bremner
of Scotland

BOBBY MOORE

BOBBY MOORE began to show what a master footballer he would be when in almost his first match in First
Division soccer, at the age of 17, he amazed the crowd by
proving he could remove the ball from the feet of opponents who prided themselves in the game of bluff and
selling a dummy. He was the junior in West Ham's
league side, but within five years he was captain of England.

Both as club and national captain, Moore succeeded
because of his ability to anticipate the flow of play,
coupled with outstanding coolness no matter how great
the crisis. Only coolness could have enabled him to play
as well as ever during the nightmare weeks in the
summer of 1970 when he was accused of stealing
jewellery from a shop in Colombia during England's
warm-up visit before the World Cup. Moore knew he
was innocent, millions of fans *believed* he was innocent,
but no matter what the law may say, in the eyes of the

world any top star is guilty until proved innocent – and it took several agonizing months before it was clearly demonstrated that Moore had been 'framed'. Many top players would have shown signs of such a strain in their play, but not Bobby.

That coolness caught the attention of Sir Alf Ramsey, England's team manager, when he began the job of building England's 1966 World Cup team. Bobby had already led West Ham to their first F.A. Cup win, in 1964, and a triumph in the European Cup-Winners' Cup. When he captained England to World Cup victory over West Germany in the final at Wembley, the only problem left for him was to find new targets to aim at.

Captaincy, and its worries, have never reduced the quality of his individual play. Moore would be the first to agree that no captain can hope to succeed if he calls for more from his men than he gives himself.

He has continued to give for more than a dozen years, with a skill and determination which not only wins matches, but also entertains.

MARY RAND

BRITAIN's 'Golden Girl of Athletics' she was called in the nineteen-sixties. She had been well known *within* athletics before 1960, but it was during the 1960 Rome Olympics that she first became front page news. She reached the final of the 80 metres hurdles, and gave hope of being able to bring off a Gold Medal for Britain in the Long Jump.

She led the qualifying round with a new British record of 20 feet 9¼ inches. What ruined her chances in the final was a faulty run-up, followed by another, so that she was unnerved by the time of her next jump and managed only 19 feet 8½ inches, eliminating herself from the last three jumps. V. Krepkina of Russia took the Gold Medal with a magnificent 20 feet 8½ inches.

During the next four years Mary's athletics career was meteoric. She scored time and again for Britain in internationals – and the range of her abilities made her a pentathlon star as well. Looking ahead to 1964, the big question was whether she could become the first British Athlete ever to win a Gold Medal for jumping in the history of the Games.

In the qualifying round, Germany's Hoffmann set the pace for the day by easily beating the 1960 record, but then Mary Rand jumped still further, even though there was a gusty wind and the run-up was soaking from a heavy downpour.

There were many uneasy eyes on Mary as the final began. Would the same thing happen as at Rome – would her nerve fail her?

It did not.

At her fifth jump Mary Rand set a new World and Olympic record of 22 feet $2\frac{1}{4}$ inches. Her two rivals, Kirszenstein of Poland and Russia's Tatyana Schelkanova, could come nowhere near this distance.

Many people looked to her to repeat her Gold Medal performance in the 1968 Olympics, but an injury during a hurdles race a few months before the Games ruined her chances, and she retired from athletics.

DONALD CAMPBELL

Sir Malcolm Campbell set world records on land and on water; his son, Donald Campbell took over the task of raising the water speed record even higher. His first attempt was on Coniston Water in Lancashire, in 1949 – ten years after the last run by his father over the same course. He failed – but bitten by the speed bug, he felt compelled to go on. In September 1956 he took out the turbo-jet engined Bluebird over the same course, and in all he broke the water speed record seven times during his eighteen years of attempts.

In 1964 he became the first man to set both world land and world water speed records in the same year. His land speed record was for conventionally powered cars – he drove his Bluebird car at 403.1 miles an hour. The water speed record, in the Bluebird boat, was 276.33 miles an hour. Both records were set in Australia.

But the danger of these fantastic speeds had already been fully proved to him. In 1960 in a land speed record attempt at the Salt Flats in Utah, he crashed when speeding at 360 miles an hour. Most men would have seen the warning light, but throughout Donald Campbell's life he seemed to be spurred on by the need to outdo his father.

But it was not a land speed record attempt which ended his life. At the beginning of 1967 he was once again at Coniston Water, determined to raise his water speed record still further. Sponsors had mostly abandoned him; they felt nothing further could be learned by the car and boat industries by record attempts. Underfinanced, and with a Bluebird boat which several experts claimed was aerodynamically unsound, he went out and made a very fast first run.

On the return run, at top speed, Bluebird suddenly leaped out of the water, somersaulted, and disintegrated. Campbell was killed instantly, ending a period of sixty years in which father and son had unceasingly sought to keep a Campbell as the fastest man on land or water.

HARVEY SMITH

At any big show-jumping meeting the world over, Harvey Smith is always one of the most fancied competitors. The list of his victories is a long one, but it is only in very recent years that the show-jumping public has become used to the idea of Harvey as a winner. For until the nineteen-sixties, the sport was dominated by cavalry officers and what used to be described as 'the landed gentry'. Plain Harvey Smith, an apprentice bricklayer in his family's building firm at Bingley in Yorkshire, kept his horses at the bottom of the back garden of his suburban house, and was a slightly unexpected choice to represent Britain in Dublin in 1957. A tough, no-nonsense Yorkshireman, he was often taken for a brother of another tough, no-nonsense Yorkshireman, the former Test bowler Fred Trueman. The experts laughed at his choice of horses; he used to buy old ones on which other riders had failed. They stopped laughing when he began to win on them.

Harvey moved to a farm high up on Ilkley Moor, where there would be no interruptions to the careful work of turning old hacks into world class jumpers. The choice of old horses was deliberate. He wanted experience and stamina, and his selections were made among horses which he felt confident were failing only because they were not getting the right handling.

His methods of preparing horses for the jumping ring have never varied. They have been firm, but fair. He believes in a close partnership between rider and horse – but with no mistake about who is the senior partner!

Nearly six feet tall, heavily muscled, and occasionally in trouble for his outspokenness, Harvey Smith has had perhaps more than his share of problems at the top in show-jumping. But those who have been infuriated by him have always forgiven him. It is not possible to stay angry with a man who on one occasion a few years ago took on the entire American team two days running – and beat them!

John Surtees (left)

JOHN SURTEES

The hospital in Ontario, Canada, issued a grim bulletin. '... It has been decided not to operate on him at the moment. He has lost a lot of blood, and his condition is critical.'

The man they were talking about was John Surtees, Britain's double champion – the man who had the distinction of being World Champion for both motor-cycle and car racing.

John Surtees had been at the top; when he opened his eyes again four days after that bulletin, he was right at the bottom again, with, ahead of him, the long struggle to win back his place in sport.

At 31, he was young enough to make a comeback. There was no question of his having reached his peak and passed it. When he crashed, he was practising for the Canadian Grand Prix, and had already emerged as one of the top qualifiers. His brakes locked at high speed, his car shed a wheel, and then rolled down an em-

bankment, overturning and pinning him underneath
it.

Other bulletins were issued as Surtees lay there in his
hospital bed. 'His injuries are so serious that it is doubt-
ful whether he will ever race again.' 'He will lack the
muscular control to handle a car at high speeds.'

Surtees did not hear about these until he was back in
London, hobbling about on sticks. His friends tried to
persuade him to give up; he had his own prosperous
garage business – surely that was enough?

For John Surtees it was not enough. In April 1966 he
was back behind the wheel once more, this time in a
brand-new Ferrari, a big four-litre machine which on
this, its first outing, was entered for the 1,000 kilometre
Monza race, one of the toughest races there is for both
men and machines.

Nobody expected him to win, but he battled his way
round 100 laps of the six mile circuit in pouring rain at
an average speed of nearly 103 miles an hour, keeping
the lead from start to finish and lapping all except four of
the other cars in the race. At the finish he was minutes
ahead of his nearest rival! Asked if he had been scared
all the time of another accident, he grinned. 'If I'd been
scared, I could never have started again.'

He had learned the lesson of wartime fighter pilots
who, dazed after a smash, were promptly sent up again in
other planes before they had time to lose their nerve. He
had applied the method to himself. It was brutal – but
effective!

PETER SNELL

New Zealand was briefly prominent in international athletics when Jack Lovelock won the 1,500 metres in the 1936 Berlin Olympics, but it was not until 1960 that this small nation of only 2½ million people produced another world-beater. This was Peter Snell. In the 800 metres final at the Rome Olympics the Belgian holder of the world record, R. Moens, was considered certain to win, but Snell, virtually an unknown, came through on the inside about forty yards from home to beat him by a fifth of a second in a new Olympic record of 1 minutes 46.3 seconds.

But four years later in Tokyo Snell was far from being an unknown. His tactics, which had astonished experts throughout the world in the years between, seemed to be to *ignore* tactics. For him no carefully calculated slow laps and pace-making, but right from the gun a killing speed which he knew he could maintain and increase but suspected others could not. In the 800 metres at Tokyo that pace was matched and surpassed for the first lap by the Kenyan, Wilson Kiprugut, who was in the lead after the first 400 metres. But there was no doubt in anyone's mind at what cost this lead was held. It appeared the Kenyan was running as if the tape was waiting at the half-way stage; the moment he was into the second lap the edge went off his speed, and Snell, with no obvious 'kick' of acceleration, simply moved past him and on to finish in 1 minute 45.1.

But an 800 metres Gold Medal was only half Snell's target. He was also in the final of the 1,500 metres, in which Britain had Alan Simpson and John Whetton, and Snell was partnered by John Davies.

It looked promising for Britain when Whetton raced past two Frenchmen who had set a very fast pace for the first lap. But then Davies took the lead for New Zealand. Snell, still well back, did not appear worried by his poor position – and the reason why became clear, for when the pacemakers' speeds were falling off, his was not. At 1,000 metres he had moved up and was shoulder to shoulder with Davies. Coming up towards the bell, Davies moved out in front again, but with the crowd yelling his name Snell continued his gradual increase in speed. It was something Davies could not match. Though comfortably in front, Snell then produced a finishing burst, one which set the crowd on its toes, and crossed the line in 3 minutes 38.1, to win by $1\frac{1}{2}$ seconds.

TOM FINNEY

THE argument can be fast and furious when the question arises of how the great soccer players of the past would fare in present day football. Clearly, some would adapt themselves, and the skill which put them at the top in their day would be just as useful nowadays, but others might not be so fortunate. Many stars of the past succeeded not only by their own merits, but by the deficiencies of their opponents.

One who might still succeed is Tom Finney, Preston North End and England outside right of the nineteen-forties and fifties. He was not a man who ran himself into the ground for the sake of success. He sweated – but only in hot weather. The Finney skill lay largely in his ability to make himself unobtrusive, so that unexpectedly he could pounce, scoop up the ball from the foot of an opponent, and then beat two more by marking time with the ball and appearing to signal a pass when he had no intention of making it. In many matches, including even internationals, for most of the game he would hardly seem to take part at all, then suddenly, at a carefully calculated moment, he would be right in the heart of the game, winkling out the ball and placing it right on the boot of the man in the best position to score.

Nearly twenty years ago at Wembley he gave one of his most typical performances, in a match against Scotland. For at least thirty minutes of the game he played no part at all, standing alone on the right wing while Sam Cox, the Scotsman whose job it was to mark him, became gradually more careless about the way he did so.

It was exactly what Finney wanted!

Out of the blue he collected the ball, weaved and tacked his way through the defence by masterly trickery, and flipped a pass across to a waiting striker timed so perfectly that a miss was impossible. Then, in the second half, he made another goal by beating Cox, taking the ball down to a spot midway between the corner flag and the near post, and then tapping it back at ground level to the penalty spot in front of three unmarked England players.

Part of his goal-making success lay in the fact that instinctively when a winger reaches the goal-line, most of the defence retreat right into the goalmouth, waiting for the ball to be centred into their midst. It was *not* centring it that gave Finney most of the 30 goals he scored in his 76 internationals!

HENRY COTTON

Henry Cotton joined the thin ranks of golf's immortals on a July afternoon in 1934. It was the British Open Championship, at Sandwich, and though beforehand Cotton had felt he was going to fail, he played a magnificent qualifying round, and in the actual championship he started with a 67, a fantastic 66, and then a 72 to stand ten strokes in front of his nearest rival.

But then came disaster. There was a twenty minutes delay in the starting time of his final round, and Cotton, already suffering from an ulcer, became physically ill with nervous strain. When he teed up at the first, everything went wrong. He could not time his drives, his approach shots went wide, and only his putting saved him from losing all he had gained. His chances of breaking 80 looked remote.

And then, at the thirteenth hole, his third shot put him ten feet from the pin. He stood looking at it, sweating with the exhaustion that comes of failure.

The crowd watched in tense silence as Cotton made his putt. Then there was a great 'Ohhhh!' of relief as it went in!

From that moment on, he recovered – to win the British Open Championship by five strokes.

His success was based on a beautifully controlled and powerful drive, accuracy with his approach shots, and complete calm on the greens. These features were never more evident than in his second Open victory, three years later at Carnoustie. A howling wind was lashing rain across the course when he went into his final round three strokes behind the leader. Cotton simply kept his head when all about him were losing theirs – and won. The war came as a serious interruption to his career, but after it he proved he was still a master by winning his third Open, in 1948, by the massive margin of five strokes!

GARY SOBERS

IN cricket, an orthodox all-rounder is a rarity. Success as an all-rounder nearly always depends on some quaint but effective scoring stroke, or a bowling technique so abnormal that batsmen do not fathom it out until after they have returned to the pavilion.

Gary Sobers is a completely orthodox pace bowler, even though his run up is more appropriate to a fast-medium delivery. And in batting, his only unorthodox stroke is his hook, which appears to depend more on wrist and perfect timing than on footwork.

At 16, he was already taking wickets for Barbados, and before he was 18 he was playing against England in a Test series – again more prominently as a bowler than as a batsman. When the Australians visited the West Indies, he was second in the bowling averages, and in 8 innings had a batting average of 38.5. The return tour was a severe setback, and the West Indies selectors must have wondered if they had made a mistake, for Gary

failed with the bat and with the ball, and it was not until
1957, when he came to England, that he proved this to
have been only temporary. The demoralizing bowling of
Laker and Lock, which in the final Test claimed so
many West Indies wickets, held no terrors for him. Six
years later on his second England tour he was greeted,
and treated, as possibly the greatest cricketer of all time.
Over the years, he has scattered cricketing records in all
directions, and been cheered by the supporters of opposing sides probably more often than any other player. It is
impossible, in any sport, to win a tribute greater than
that.

BOBBY LOCKE

ARTHUR D'ARCY LOCKE of South Africa dominated British golf for longer than most home professionals care to remember. Tall, plump, double-chinned, he looked more like a cheerful amateur out for a gentle nine holes to settle his lunch, but for year after year he proved himself to be consistently a great player.

But not always a popular one. He would not hurry. No matter what the situation or the importance of the occasion, Bobby Locke took his time. Sometimes this may have helped him to win, for other players became so overwrought while waiting for him to finish a hole that it distracted them from their game!

But where he showed his mastery was in his magnificent composure when his game was going badly. In 1950 he was defending the British Open title, which he had won the previous year. Conditions at Troon were perfect; dry weather had made the fairways smooth.

Perhaps it looked a shade too good; Locke knew there were many rivals whose game was at its best in perfect conditions. He could not afford to drop a stroke at any stage of the four rounds. But all went well for him on the first day, and he was round in 69. On the second day he started out equally well, and was one under par after four holes. But then, at the short fifth, Locke's drive missed the green. Trying to pitch the ball up to the pin, he then underhit it, and went straight into a bunker.

The bunker was a difficult one, and it took him two strokes to get out. He eventually holed out in six.

To a professional, the Open Championship is not only

an important cash prize, but a prestige victory on which
the chance for future successes depend. Locke was now
all set to lose, and lose badly. Most players would have
gone to pieces completely, swamped by thoughts of 'if
only', but not Locke. His only reaction was to step up his
game, pare a stroke off his score for each of the next few
holes – and then go on to play superb third and fourth
rounds to retain the title!

WARWICK ARMSTRONG

Warwick Armstrong, Australia's massive twenty stone cricket captain of the early days of the present century, never lost a Test match in a career that lasted nearly 22 years. His huge bulk looked quite unsuitable for consistent batting, clever fielding, and an ability to keep up a high standard of slow bowling hour after hour.

In the years before the First World War he achieved spectacular performances for his country both on home grounds and in England, but his battles on the field were equalled by those in the pavilion! There were rows with the Test selectors, rows with the Australian cricket authorities, and the rows continued after the war. While against England in Sydney he was hitting the ball so hard no England fieldsmen could stop it, let alone catch it, there were constant conspiracies to have him dropped from the Test team.

The climax came when he was dropped from Victoria's team against MCC at Melbourne. A huge crowd held a protest meeting outside the ground, and eventually the cricket officials had to apologize and reinstate him – more important still, they had to forgive him for past rows and make a fresh start.

His return, in the next Test, was greeted by a standing ovation from the packed spectators. Australia were quickly in trouble but Warwick went in and got them out of it by scoring 123 not out.

In the next Test series, in England, Australia won the Ashes after only eight days of cricket – two for the First Test, and three each for the Second and Third! But there were rows again – over rules, over tactics, and over conditions of the tour, and though the team played 34 matches without defeat, back in Australia there were fierce arguments about whether they had all been genuinely sporting victories.

The arguments still rage over whether he was a fair-minded sportsman. But that he was a brilliant cricketer there can be no doubt.

ROD LAVER

MORE than twenty years ago on the dusty, sun-scorched tennis courts of northern Queensland a farmer's son began to make a name for himself. He had the right background, for both his parents and his two brothers were all tennis players, of a standard high enough to make it worth while for the whole family to travel hundreds of miles to take part in tournaments.

But Rod Laver was soon picked out by the experts as being something more than just a good club-standard player. He was sent to Brisbane for first class coaching, and there he was noticed by Australia's top tennis officials, who began to see him as a possible successor to Lew Hoad in the Davis Cup and Wimbledon.

They were soon proved right. He turned out to be the most successful left hander in modern tennis, reaching the final at Wimbledon in two successive years, and then going on to win it in 1961 and 1962.

The description of Laver which fits him best is relentless. Perhaps this is shown best not in his Wimbledon finals matches, but in some of the quarter and semi-final battles on the way to the top. A quarter final against Manuel Santana in 1962, when Laver was defending the title, began with the Spaniard playing a fast and energetic game which won him the first set and took him to a 5–1 lead in the second. Facing this, most players would have lost heart. But Laver played his usual game, keeping absolutely steady and unruffled, while Santana burned himself out. Eventually he knew the Spaniard would have to relax – and the moment he did, Laver's pressure broke service to make it 5–2. He broke it again to reach 5–4. Santana then regained his concentration, and attacked hard, to put Laver in the dangerous position of trailing love–30 on his own service. Laver's reply was to move up to the net and return a Santana lob with the handle of his racket and make it 15–30. A swerving serve came back just inside the line; somehow, with his back to the net and badly-balanced on one foot, Laver half-volleyed a winner.

That broke Santana's morale, and from this point on the match was never in doubt. For throughout this dangerous spell, Laver had never looked flustered, never looked anything but a man who expected to win.

And, as usual, he did.

COLIN BELL

MANCHESTER CITY were lucky in the late nineteen-sixties with a youngster who within months of arrival showed he might become one of the greatest soccer players of all time.

Colin Bell, one of the new style players able to perform brilliantly in any position on the field, joined City from Bury in 1966. Hair flying wild in the wind, he was quickly popular with the crowds at Maine Road, not only because of his ability to make a difficult move look simple, but also because of the amount of energy he put into the game. One expert described him as playing a ninety minute match as though it was only ten minutes each way, but still ending with the speed and alertness with which he started!

Manchester City's League Championship win, their F.A. Cup triumph, and success in the League Cup as well, has depended largely on the consistency of their attack, and the almost telepathic communication between Bell, Francis Lee, and the others involved in the moves which have so frequently left defences baffled. Flexibility in attack – the new look in soccer – had already been pioneered by many teams which had abandoned the rigid formations of the past, but it was the ability of City's attack to act in unison right from one penalty area to the other which gave them the ten per cent 'edge' over so many of their opponents.

Bell has been the key figure in this attack throughout, establishing himself as one of the first great players of club soccer's second hundred years. Already, though only in his early twenties, he has been forecast as England's great hope for the future in World Cup football, with a career comparable to that of Bobby Charlton or Pclc.

KING HENRY VIII

THE great all-rounders in sport date back thousands of years, to the Greek athletes who could run, throw, or wrestle with equal skill. Britain's first all-rounder whose exploits are known was King Henry VIII. The game of Real, or Royal, Tennis, had been imported from France, and at London's Hampton Court Palace, built in 1530, can be seen the court in which Henry VIII played for a year or two. It was in the earlier years of the sixteenth century that he achieved a reputation as a huntsman, a keen follower of horseracing, no mean athlete as a hammer-thrower, and very able at fencing.

A sport in which he excelled was archery, a skill which was becoming obsolete in war but increasingly popular as a recreation

Bowls was another of his interests. This was played at Whitehall, but it is believed the game differed considerably from what it is today. And though many records say that golf was not imported into England from north of the Border until the arrival on the throne of King James I, others maintain that it arrived in the early part of the sixteenth century, and was another of Henry VIII's pastimes.

Britain had gone through several centuries in which any leisure activity not connected with training for war had been frowned upon by authority; suddenly here was a king who unknowingly was the first Minister for Sport. The events in which he competed quickly gained popularity, and the fact that most major sports were pioneered by Britain must to some degree be his responsibility!

NEIL HARVEY

THE ability to hit runs is a talent common to thousands of cricketers, but scoring fast against attacking bowlers is a skill which separates the masters from the also-rans! It was in the 1958–9 Test series against England that Neil Harvey showed which category was his.

It was the Second Test. England had made 259 – an inadequate first innings on paper, but one which on the huge Melbourne ground designed for Australian Rules Football might just be too big a target for Australia. Fours are not easily hit on this immense oval 200 yards in diameter.

Australia's first wicket was taken by the England opening bowler Brian Statham with only 11 on the board, and this brought together Harvey and McDonald. It is an indication of how far away the boundary seems at Melbourne that McDonald batted four hours for 47 without scoring a single four! Harvey, at the other end, soon demonstrated that fours *were* possible. Even though England's skipper Peter May rang the changes in his bowling time and again, Harvey hit ten fours in making 60 by close of play.

Next morning May set a defensive field, with defensive bowling, and waited for Harvey to become impatient.

He misjudged his man. Harvey matched guile for guile, treating the bowling with extreme caution until the bowlers grew tired.

And then he struck. He opened up so suddenly that the bored crowds leaped to their feet. On a fast outfield his strokes were almost unstoppable, and though he lost McDonald with the total at 126, caught at slip off Statham, with O'Neill as his new partner he survived the new ball. O'Neill was not at his best, and batted defensively, leaving Harvey to go for the runs. Australia were now near the England total, and there was no way in which May could block the gaps in the field. Harvey steered the ball neatly through the field, reaching the boundary with almost every stroke, and scored 167 before a full toss from Loader slipped under his bat.

If ever there was one man's match, this was it. Australia made 308, and the England batsmen, convinced that what Harvey could do, they could do also, were rapidly disillusioned by being dismissed for 87. Australia then hit the winning 42 for the loss of two wickets.

CHRIS CHATAWAY

'I SHALL retire,' Chris Chataway said firmly in reply to those who asked him what he would do after the 1956 Melbourne Olympic Games. 'I shall remain interested, of course, but I shan't run any more. Imagine what it must feel like to watch your performances slowly getting worse as the years go by!'

For a man who has broken world records, perhaps sudden and complete retirement is best. And Chris Chataway's cup of triumph during his seven great years had been filled to the brim, though in a rather curious way.

Chris ran a mile in 4 minutes 42 during his schooldays in Dorset, and six years later he set up a world record for the 5,000 metres, but in between these two events he earned himself strange titles such as 'The Pusher', and 'The Great Mr Second'. He got those through his selfless assistance to Roger Bannister and John Landy in conquering the four minute mile, and by some heart-breakingly narrow defeats in the three miles. Chris was not ready for a four minute mile when Bannister started to plan his attempt – yet he gave his wholehearted co-operation even though he had no hope of achieving it himself. He finished nearly eight seconds behind Bannister, but it was his pushing that helped Bannister to succeed. For the first half mile, and into the back straight of the third lap, the leader was Chris Brasher, running at a brisk pace, and followed closely by Bannister, with Chataway almost breathing down Bannister's neck in third place. As was inevitable, Brasher as pacemaker outran himself, and dropped back. Promptly Chris Chataway shot past Bannister to take over the lead.

At the start of the final lap, Chataway was still slightly in front, but then, with 250 yards to go, Bannister opened up his stride and pulled well out in front of his pacemaker to break the tape in 3 minutes 59.4 seconds.

Only a few weeks later, at Turku in Finland, Chris Chataway carried out the same gallant work of taking second place after pushing John Landy all the way in his attempt that lowered the record to 3 minutes 58 seconds. And Landy's first tribute was to Chataway. 'If he hadn't been chasing me round the track, the record wouldn't have gone!'

The 5,000 metres world record was his eventual reward. But his athletics career is remembered even more for those two occasions when he ran not for himself, but for others.

ALLAN CLARKE

ALLAN CLARKE has been a controversial player ever since he first came into professional soccer. At Walsall, even when he was scoring goals for them, the local crowd viewed him with suspicion, considering him a player who cared more for himself than for the team. There was much the same verdict at Fulham. Later at Leicester there were sneers that Clarke was in soccer only for the money – particularly his share of transfer fees.

What few people seemed to bear in mind, when the same criticism was made at the time of his move to Leeds, was that Clarke is a 'finisher', with the job of turning mere chances into goals – a job in which speed and immaculate timing are essential. When Leeds paid £165,000 for him in the summer of 1969 they were paying this high price for a quick brain, and feet which could save tenths of seconds. The career of a man whose success depends on these factors is short, shorter even than that of a swimming star. Two or three seasons right at the top may well be 'the lot' for this lean six-footer who snatched goals out of situations where in theory the defence should win. Quick moneymaking *has* to be high on his list of priorities, for the step from First to Fourth Division football can be sudden.

In the 1969–70 season Clarke learned from Don Revie at Leeds the art of curbing the criticism of the crowds, by showing on and off the field that he was a team-man. His goals for Leeds – the 20 which made him the club's top scorer in League matches, as well as those along the road to the Cup Final – were scored not so much as a lone opportunist but as climaxes to moves begun in midfield by his skipper Billy Bremner and the resourceful Jackie Charlton, and carried to the goalmouth by close collaboration involving his colleagues in the attack.

CASSIUS CLAY

On the night of 25th February, 1964 at Miami Beach, Sonny Liston failed to answer the bell at the start of the seventh round against a young, fast-moving boxer of perfect physique combined with a powerful punch. Cassius Clay – later to call himself Muhammed Ali – was the new king of the heavyweights.

And king of the loudmouths. When they fought the return bout three months later, and Clay knocked out Liston in only 1 minute and 42 seconds, there were more boasts than punches.

His defences of the title were always preceded by interviews in which he described in detail just how great he was, and just how much of a victory he would have. The only justification was that it was all true! He stopped Floyd Patterson in 1965 in the second round; in 1966 beat George Chuvalo on points, stopped Britain's Henry Cooper in the sixth, knocked out Brian London in the third, and then in seven hectic months beat Karl

Mildenberger, Cleveland Willams, Ernie Terrell, and Zora Folley.

But suddenly in 1967 it all ended. Clay objected violently to American war policy in Vietnam, and refused to be called up for military service. The boxing authorities in America stripped him of his world title, and there began a long wrangle over whether or not he should serve a prison sentence.

It was not until late in 1970 that Clay was able to enter the ring again – and meanwhile there had been a new world championship struggle, and a new champion had been created.

For Muhammed Ali, the road back to the top, after three inactive years, involved regaining fitness, speed, and endurance. His ambition – to do what no man had ever done before, regain the world heavyweight title. But however that struggle might end, no boxer or boxing fan could ever deny that this was the most impressive, and most entertaining, top class boxer in the history of the ring.